Gourmet Weeds

CYGNET BROWN & KERRY KELLEY

Ozark Grannies' Secrets LLC

GOURMET WEEDS

ISBN: 979-8-9879153-0-1
LCCN: 2023935066

Publisher's Cataloging-in-Publication data
Names: Kelley, Kerry, author. | Brown, Cygnet, author.
Title: Ozark grannies' secrets : gourmet weeds / Kerry Kelley; Cygnet
Brown.
Description: Includes bibliographical references and index. | Alton, MO:
Ozark Grannies' Secrets LLC,
2023.
Identifiers: ISBN: 979-8-9879153-0-1
Subjects: LCSH Cooking (Wild foods) | Cooking--Ozark Mountains Region. |
Wild plants, Edible--United
States--Identification. | Cookbooks. | BISAC COOKING / Specific Ingredi-
ents / Natural Foods | COOKING
/ Regional & Ethnic / American / Southern States
Classification: LCC QK98.5.U6 .K45 2023 | DDC 581.6/32/0973--dc23

ACKNOWLEDGEMENTS

Acknowledgements

We Acknowledge and thank Sharon Hudson for allowing us to use her recipe "Ozark Style Gumbo".

DEDICATION PAGE

This Book is Dedicated To

Our husbands—Steve Kelley and Jeff Brown who have graciously allowed us to follow our passions.

CONTENTS

WELCOME TO OZARK GRANNIES' SECRETS

public domain clipart

Welcome to our Ozarks! Whether you're a tourist just passing through, a newbie to the area, or someone who has lived in the Ozarks for a long time, we want to share with you an aspect of the Ozarks that is near and dear to our hearts. In this book, we of Ozark Grannies' Secrets want to share some of our knowledge of forageable foods with you.

So, what will we at Ozark Grannies' Secrets share with you today in the first book in our series? Grab a glass of sweet tea, scooch up to the table, and pay attention to our amazing yarns. We want to entertain you with stories and share how you can make larruping good Ozark dishes with forageable greens, fruits, vegetables, and nuts to stretch your food dollars using some of the good foods that are available to us here in the Ozarks.

We started this book by pondering what we might have wanted to know as new homesteaders, and how to take stock of some of the resources that are already growing here. Let's say we've brought along a few kitchen staples and want to round out our meals with some of these readily available edibles.

At the same time, it's our Ozarks' way to keep an extra meal or two handy in the freezer for those neighbors in need, whether through the loss of a loved one, family sickness, or misfortune. Many of us were taught to be "our brother's keeper" and we'll treat others like family with the gift of a homemade dish and maybe a blackberry cobbler.

You'll find there's an abundance of information to chew on in this little volume, and we're proud glad you'uns are here.

Cygnet's Story

"My first trip through the Ozarks in 1979 convinced me that this was where I wanted to live. The wide variety of wildflowers and other plants blew my mind. I loved the fact that many of the houses here were smaller homes, and there was just something about the atmosphere of the area that told me that this was where I belonged.

In 1984, I bought my first piece of land here through a company that sold land on a land contract. Land contract, I discovered later, although easier to obtain than using traditional loans, is not always the best buy. I think it's better to go through an owner finance situation or a traditional real estate agency."

Kerry's Story

"My Ozarks history began in 1983. Land prices and taxes being so much more affordable than in my native California, plus extended family in Missouri, brought me here. Two-lane roads, tiny villages of friendly people, and clean clear water kept me here!

I gathered and learned to recognize many forageables while living on the West Coast and was happy to find many of the same plants growing here in the Ozarks. Since then, I've learned many more and continue to do so. We hope you're inspired to join us on this wonderful journey and follow us in our adventures!"

The Region We Call Home

We are proud to live in the Ozarks. The word Ozark is believed to be a corruption of the French Aux Arc, meaning '**bend in the river**', describing a large bend in the Arkansas River. History claims it was the name of a French trading post among the Quapaw people and was established in the region in the 1700s.

Our Ozarks cover Missouri mostly south of the Missouri River, northern Arkansas, and extreme eastern Oklahoma, as well as a sliver of eastern Kansas. Although the population of most Ozark towns is still small, the number of tourists who visit each year is believed to be numbered in the millions.

Here you can explore caves, wet weather streams, and a multitude of blue springs and rivers. Underneath our feet are huge sources of water endlessly flowing through the Ozarks' unique karst topography. Water often escapes to the surface from these underground aquafers via springs. On the surface, strange depressions in the landscape, which we call sinkholes, hint at collapsed underground caverns. As erosion wears away the land above ground, steep limestone cliffs become visible.

The Ozarks are home to an amazing assortment of plant and animal life. Imagine hardwood forests, pine groves, cedar glades, Prairie remnants, river bottoms, and bald knobs, all spread out in our roughly 47,000 square miles (about half the area of Arizona).

The stony hills and hollers make it an ideal area for finding many forageable foods because excessive cultivation has not depleted the variety of plant species. The wild and beautiful Ozarks are essentially not suitable for growing most commercial crops. However, in generations past, many local families grew sizable acres of corn and cotton for themselves and as a source of income.

Prickly pear cacti and paw paws grow near one another in white oak forests. Many plants (and some animals) are only found in the Ozarks. Plants that prefer more northern climates are found near caves. Desert species grow on the dry rocky glades. In the spring, the Ozarks explode with springtime blooms like bloodroot, trout lily, jack in the pulpit, and violets that live a short life before the onset of warm weather and tree leaf growth. In the summer, roadsides burst with echinacea, butterfly weed, wild carrot, and daisy-like Jerusalem artichokes, and many other wildflowers.

It's, without a doubt, a wonderful place for foraging for wild edibles.

A Word of Caution

While foraging for wild edibles is fun and educational, and can be a wonderful family adventure, identification of these listed here and in future volumes is extremely important. Not only should you make sure the plant, nut, or seed is wholesome through your own added research, but also that they haven't been exposed to roadside chemicals or other chemical controls in pastures or gardens. Always determine that your harvesting environment is safe and clean and that you're not sharing it with sneaky snakes or other wood folks who're there first.

We hope you never need it, but in case you do, here's an important number to keep around. Post a copy of it on your refrigerator. **In case of exposure or any adverse effects of ingestion, contact a Poison Control Center (800-222-1222)**

This volume is for the reference and amusement of our readers only, and we encourage you'uns to consult an expert in the identification of all the plants listed before consuming any foraged foods. We've made every effort to present accurate information, however, neither the authors, editors nor publisher assumes any responsibility for errors or omissions or any consequence from the application of this information.

Ozark Grannies' Safety and Etiquette Recommendations

Here at Ozark Grannies' Secrets, we're not going to tell you that you can't do something. That never works because there will be people who will argue with what someone else says that they must do. Ozark folks are especially resistant to someone else telling them what to do. Therefore, we are offering a few recommendations that we believe are beneficial to you and will help keep the Ozarks as beautiful and natural as the region.

As you'll notice, we don't have photographs of the various plants in the book. We did that on purpose. We don't want you thinking that you could compare our pictures to what is growing in your yard and nearby field or forest and think that's good enough. We don't include them on purpose because we don't want you to mistake a poisonous plant for a nonpoisonous one. For instance, yarrow, wild carrots, and poison hemlock have a very similar look, but poison hemlock will kill you.

Rather than depending on our book for pictures identifying plants, we suggest that you consult someone experienced in foraging for wild foods. If you know someone who has been foraging and eating plants in the wild for years, that person is likely to be your best resource. Other professional resources include your local conservation or extension office. Online apps can also be a useful resource. (We've included a few suggestions on page 109 entitled Resources.)

1. When you are sure of what you want to harvest, we recommend that you pick no more than one-third of a plot of any specific plant type. We hope that you will leave the other two-thirds for the animals that might depend on the plant

and have some to grow on so that the next person can reap the benefits as well. In addition, you'll know where there's a patch growing whenever you want more of that plant.

2. Be aware and cautious about where you are getting your foraged foods. Avoid areas where plants have been sprayed with chemicals like herbicides and pesticides. Ingesting these chemicals can be very harmful.No matter where you forage, be sure to wash your foraged foods before processing them to eat.

3. For the most nutritional value from your foraged food, use it at once or as soon as possible.

4. Avoid mixing several varieties of foraged foods that you have never tried before. For example, if you have never eaten dandelions, clovers, plantain, and violets don't try all of them in the same salad at the same time. Try one at a time so if you have an allergic reaction, you'll know which one is the likely culprit.

5. In the same vein, be careful that when you're gathering your forageable foods you don't touch other poisonous plants. Remember the old adage: "Three leaves leave them be."

6. Lastly, if you chance upon a fence or property corner that isn't yours, in other words, someone else's land, be sure to ask permission! Remember "good fences make good neighbors", and many people will gladly give you permission to respectfully wander on their land looking for forageable treasures.

Rest assured the first volume of *Gourmet Weeds* is a labor of love, and we hope to encourage some curiosity, love of the outdoors, and wonderment of the bounty of the useful plants all around us.

What to Know About Us in the Ozarks

If you are new to the Ozarks, there are some things you need to know about us. We're a bit skeptical about people who want to change us. We like being individuals and we don't like people telling us that their way is better than the way we've been doing things. Some of us can make your lives miserable, but if you respect us, we'll respect you.

The Tale of the Realtor and His Prospects

We've been known to "milk" people who are ignorant of our ways too. Once there was a real estate agent who was taking a couple around looking at various properties to buy. The couple looked and looked and finally they found a piece of property that they loved except the property was covered with rocks. When the wife commented about all the rocks, the real estate agent picked up one of them from the ground and showed them the moisture under the rock. "It gets mighty dry here in the summer, so we use them to conserve moisture in the soil," he said.

The couple nodded and agreed that it was a good thing and agreed to purchase the property. On their way back to the real estate office to complete the deal, they passed a group of farmers putting rocks into a tractor bucket. When the couple questioned the agent about the activity, the agent leaned over and whispered, "Shhh, I think they are stealing them."

The Story of the Texan in the Ozarks

We don't like it when other people try to show us up either. For instance, there was a guy from a small town here in the Ozarks who went to pick up a friend from Texas at the airport to visit his homestead.

On the way down the highway, there was a cow at the side of the road. The friend from Texas asked. "What's that?"

"Why, that's a cow," our rural friend said.

"Well, we have cows bigger than that in Texas."

They went off the main highway onto a two-lane road where they saw a dog going across the road. Again, the Texan asked what the identity of the animal was.

The Ozarkian answered. "Why, that's a dog."

"We have dogs bigger than that," said the Texan.

The Ozarkian turned his truck from the two-lane state road onto a dirt county road. As he drove down the road, a snapping turtle was crossing the road.

"What is THAT?" the Texan asked.

"Oh, that? That's a tick."

What is an Ozark Granny?

Now that you know something about the Ozarks and how we do things around here, you probably want to know the answer to the question of "What is an Ozark Granny?"

An Ozark Granny is often referred to as an older woman who handles the home births of the backwoods families that didn't have access to or just don't have a fondness for hospital care. However, Ozark Grannies were and still are much more than that and we are referring to that extended definition when we call ourselves—and anyone whose stories we tell—Ozark Grannies.

Ozark Grannies are the women with the knowledge not just of midwifery, but of the old ways in general. These women could make a meal of what they could find in their backyards or pantry shelves or woodsheds and knew how to heal using methods that were common to the area using home remedies. We won't be getting into that part this time. We're mostly just talking about how she finds food to fill the bellies of her family and guests.

In our book series, it is our intention to include not just stories, but also recipes and topics of different things that an Ozark Granny might have had in her recipe book or at least in her head. We want to get that recipe written down so that future generations can have access to that recipe too!

An Ozark Granny knows that she can make delectable meals equal to those found in gourmet restaurants. She knows she has secret ingredients disguised as weeds hidden in her lawn, the fence line behind her house, and in the rows between her garden vegetables.

In this first book, we've made it a point to include many recipes that each of the originators of the series has, in fact, tested and served to our folks. Others are from family cookbooks, word-of-mouth recipes, and interesting dishes we've yet to forage and cook up. In future books, we hope to include similar recipes and of course, their stories, from other Grannies we meet around the Ozarks.

Let's begin our exploration of forageable Ozarkian cuisine with the main ingredients of a salad and potherbs-Greens.

~ 2 ~

OZARK FORAGEABLE GREENS

Public Domain Clipart

A multitude of edible greens grows in the Ozarks. You'll probably find a lot of them in your backyard, along roadsides, and along forest paths. Remember to choose greens that haven't been sprayed with toxic chemicals and wash them thoroughly before using. Greens will keep a day or two in the refrigerator but remember that the nutritional value of those greens decreases quickly after cutting.

Asparagus (Asparagus Officinalis)

Let's start with this easily recognizable garden vegetable. These can be found poking up through the weeds of old garden sites behind many old and abandoned homes early in the growing season. Its folk name is sparrow grass, I'm guessing because these little birds help to drop "fly-over" seeds. It is so easily naturalized you might have already seen it growing in the most unexpected places. I suppose it will continue to spread and earn the status of a forageable. It's very easily transplanted into your garden row, just leave enough crown to continue to thrive right where you find it. Remember Granny's rule: Only take one-third of what you find.

Asparagus Casserole

INGREDIENTS

3 pounds of asparagus spears, cut into bite-sized pieces.
Two 10.5-ounce cans of cream of celery soup
One 6-ounce container of French-fried onions
Preheat the oven to 350 degrees.
Par-boil the asparagus until tender-and crisp

INSTRUCTIONS

In a 6-inch-by-8-inch casserole dish that's about 2 inches deep, gently slide out the asparagus in three orderly clumps.

Gently shake the pan to make a solid layer of asparagus. The asparagus spears should be parallel to the short side of the casserole dish.

Empty the two cans of cream of celery soup on top of the asparagus and spread it to form the next solid layer. Completely cover the asparagus.

Place the casserole in the preheated oven and bake until the cream of celery soup starts bubbling up the sides (about 30 to 40 minutes).

Pull the casserole briefly out of the oven and make a very generous layer of the French-fried onions over the whole casserole. Bake another 8-10 minutes to crisp the onions.
***

Granny's Wonderful Egg Casserole

INGREDIENTS

6 farm eggs
6 robust spears of asparagus, boiled and chopped,
1 loaf of white bread,
4 cups milk,
1 pound pork sausage of your choice,
1 pound cheddar cheese, grated,
Spices of oregano, rosemary, or thyme if you wish, to taste.

INSTRUCTIONS

Cut the crusts off each slice of the bread, and cut each slice into eighths. Layer a greased 9 X 13 baking dish with the slices. Thoroughly crumble and cook the sausage and layer half on the bread. Add half the asparagus. Top with half the cheese and repeat a second time. Whisk the eggs and milk together, adding spices if you like, and pour over the layered dish. Refrigerate overnight and bake at 350 degrees for about 45 minutes, or until golden brown on top.

Chickweed (Stellaria media)

Common chickweed has tiny round hairless leaves and a single row of hairs along the stems. This edible plant is a short-lived perennial that grows from taproots that sprawl in different directions. It is found primarily in the early spring and often in late fall months here in the Ozarks. Chickweed has a mild flavor and is never bitter, unlike poke or dandelion.

Common chickweed leaves can be eaten raw in a salad or chopped and added to dishes like soups, eggs, pasta, or pizza recipes.

Chickweed can also be blended into dips like pesto or hummus. Here's a recipe for a curry using chickweed.

Chickweed Curry (mild)

INGREDIENTS

> 3 tablespoons olive oil
> 1 teaspoon cumin seeds
> 2 teaspoons mustard seeds
> 1 teaspoon turmeric
> 4 cups chickweed
> 1 tablespoon lemon juice
> 1 tablespoon soy sauce

INSTRUCTIONS

Heat oil in a frying pan. Add seeds, stir, and cook for two minutes. Stir in turmeric and cook for another minute. Turn off the heat. Add chopped chickweed, lemon juice, and soy sauce. Stir well and serve immediately.

Clover, Red (Trifolium pratense)

Caution: *Those allergic to the clover should not use clover in any form.*

Red clover Is a legume like peas and beans. This plant can be eaten raw or cooked. Cut the leaves and flowers the day before the plant is in full bloom. Avoid dried-out and diseased parts of the plant. Not that they will harm you. They just won't taste good. Rinse the plant with cold water to remove dirt and debris. Rinse it again just to be sure you didn't miss anything. To increase edibility, remove stems using scissors. You can eat fresh red cover in salads and wraps. You can add uncooked clover to increase the nutritional value of the soup. You can also steam the leaves and flowers to eat as a side dish or mix them with other cooked greens. You can also use red clover flower petals as a garnish for ice cream, and the red clover leaves as a garnish for fish or chicken.

Red clover flowers can be dried and ground into flour. You can mix it with equal parts white flour to help extend the life of your pantry.

Got a sweet tooth? You can also make red clover syrup. Here's the recipe.

***

Red Clover Syrup

INGREDIENTS

    4 cups Fresh Clover Flowers
    4 cups water
    ½ sliced orange or lemon (optional)

INSTRUCTIONS

Combine 4 cups of fresh red clover flowers and 4 cups of water in a pot and allow them to simmer for 20 minutes. Take your pot off the stove and allow it to sit overnight. In the morning, strain the liquid and add 4 cups of sugar and ½ of a sliced orange or lemon. Allow the mixture to sit on low heat for several hours until you have the right consistency of syrup.

Want a unique flavored tea? How about a cup of red clover tea?

***

Red Clover Tea

INGREDIENTS
4 cups boiling water,
1 cup fresh or dried red clover flowers,
2 tablespoons of mint,
Honey and/or lemon (optional)

INSTRUCTIONS

Bring 4 cups of water to a boil and then remove it from the heat. Add 1 cup of fresh or dried red clover flowers and 2 tablespoons of mint. Allow the flowers and mint and steep for 10 minutes. Pour the liquid into a tea strainer and strain the mixture into a mug or another pot. You can add honey or lemon.

For a spin on the classic potato soup, here's some red clover soup.

***

Red Clover Soup

INGREDIENTS

2 cups Fresh Red Clover Flowers
1 Tablespoon butter,
1 Cup cubed potatoes,
¼ cup tahini (or peanut butter),
1 cup water,
Favorite spices like parsley, sage, or rosemary to taste.

INSTRUCTIONS

Sauté 2 cups of fresh red clover flowers with a tablespoon of butter until they are golden brown. If you don't want to sauté, blend red clover flowers in your processor before simmering. Add 1 cup of cubed potatoes, 1/4 cup of tahini (or peanut butter), and 1 cup of water. Allow the mixture to simmer for 40 minutes. Add your favorite spices (like parsley, sage, and rosemary) to taste.

White Dutch Clover (trifolium repens)

White clover, a native to Europe and Central Asia, is a common spring plant in most yards. This clover's common names are Honeysuckle Clover, Lodi Clover, Ladino Clover, Dutch Clover, White Clover, Dutch White Clover, and White Sweet Clover. The flowers can be added to salads and Fresh leaves can be added to salads, cooked as leafy greens, and added to soups and sauces.

White clover flour (made of dried, ground clover flowers) can be sprinkled on cooked foods like boiled rice.

Here's another delicious way to try your early spring clover harvest.

Steamed Clover Greens and Blossoms

INGREDIENTS

  3 cups fresh clover and blossoms
  3 Tablespoons butter
  3 Tablespoons water or broth

INSTRUCTIONS

Pick about 3 cups of fresh clover and blossoms. Melt 3 tablespoons of butter in a skillet (preferably cast iron) and add your clover along with 3 tablespoons of water or broth. Cover and cook on low heat for several minutes, or until tender. Salt and pepper to taste and enjoy. Granny says, "Don't eat too much at a time now, or you'll bloat up like a mule on spring grass!" Easy does it!

Common Dandelion ((Taraxacum officinale)

Rumor has it that if you pick the seed head and blow on it three times, the remaining seeds will tell the time, future children, money in the bank, and life expectancy! Whether that is true or not, doing so will no doubt ensure an abundance of next year's dandelions!

If you have a yard, you no doubt have dandelions growing in it. If you learn to enjoy eating dandelions, you will almost always have something to eat. No wonder dandelions are hailed as the King of Potherbs! Dandelion greens are rich in vitamins, A, B, C, E, and K. They also have iron, potassium, magnesium, and calcium. Polyphenols in the leaves fight inflammation in the body. Cook the leaves as you would any other greens, or enjoy the young, early leaves raw in salads.

Dandelion roots are a particularly good source of fiber. You can eat the roots fresh, make tea with them, or dry them for future use.

To dry dandelion roots, chop them up into smaller pieces when fresh and then dry them.

You can also eat the yellow flowers before they go to seed. They are tasty dipped in tempura and deep fried.

If you're looking for an easy way to introduce your people to foraged fixins, try this!

Spring Dandelion Salad Fixin's

First making sure the patch hasn't been sprayed with pesticides, cut, and wash enough dandelion for about 4 servings. Toss in your large bowl with 2-3 chopped hard-boiled eggs. You may use any dressing you prefer or try one of these.

***

Granny's Dressing

INGREDIENTS

3 tablespoons virgin olive oil
1 tablespoon apple cider vinegar
salt and pepper to taste,
A dollop of stone-ground mustard

INSTRUCTIONS

Whisk and serve.

***

Red Dirt Dressing

INGREDIENTS

¼ cup virgin olive oil
2 tablespoons Miracle Whip-type salad dressing
2 ½ tablespoons apple cider vinegar
salt & pepper to taste ½ teaspoon mustard
½ teaspoon paprika

INSTRUCTIONS

Mix all ingredients together, whisk, and serve.
***

Hoe Cakes a la Dandelion

INSTRUCTIONS

Gather a cup or two of nice dandelion blossoms,
Trim off most of the stem but leave a bit so as to hold the blossom together.
Wash and drain.
Use your favorite pancake recipe or mix, adding about a tablespoon or so of sugar and the blossoms. Fry up as usual, use plenty of grease to crisp them up real nice.

Orange Daylily (Hemerocallis fulva)

Do take time to learn about and enjoy Mother Nature's grocery store! The day lily is justifiably many foragers' favorite edible. Although it is originally a domesticated plant, it's now a naturalized escapee you'll find statewide in fields, roadsides, railroads, and moist, wooded habitats.

Daylilies can be harvested four times during the year. The first harvest takes place in early spring when the tasty and tender young foliage first appears. At this time, you can cut the 3- to 5-inch outer leaves from their grassy clump, taking care not to damage the flowering stalks. These greens taste similar to creamed onions when simmered or stir-fried in oil or butter.

One easy recipe to wet your whistle:

Daylily Stir Fry

INGREDIENTS

4 ounces (or ½ cup per person) of daylily shoots,
1-4 tablespoons virgin olive oil,
1 clove garlic, minced,
½ tsp. sesame oil,
½ tsp. soy sauce.

INSTRUCTIONS

Gather the green shoots early in Spring, and separate them into individual leaves. Wash well and drain.

Fry up the garlic in oil, stirring so as not to stick.

Add the shoots and stir, wilting them all down.

Add the soy sauce and sesame oil.

Toss and serve.

This plant is even more versatile. You'll find more uses for daylily in the Ozark Forageable Vegetables section in this book. For more about eating daylilies find them in the Forageable Vegetable section of this book on pages 83-84)

Dock (Rumex sp.)

There are several species worth mentioning, each has a slightly different appearance, all equally abundantly nutritious.

The first mention goes to **curly dock (Rumex crispus)** also known as yellow dock. This one sports that tall, brown seed stock that appears from fall into winter that almost everyone is familiar with. The early spring growth leaves are delicious paired with pokeweed greens, usually boiled in several waters and seasoned with bacon grease and vinegar. An old-fashioned treat for sure!

Next is **sour dock (Rumex acetosella)** AKA sheep sorrel, field sorrel) is more low-growing and dainty. Leaves and stems have a delightful lemony zing to nibble on the trail or add to cooked dishes for a nice tart element. Cooking will reduce the oxalates if you happen to be sensitive to those compounds.

Larruping Dock

Larruping is an Old South description of exceptionally scrumptious country-cooked food.

Most spring greens like dock can be boiled in two waters, that is; boil once, change to fresh water, and boil again. Season to your own taste with salt, pepper, butter, and a dash of vinegar. Try adding cooked crumbled bacon and stir in a chopped hard-boiled egg. Try using sparingly in any recipe that calls for a bit of boiled greens in omelets, wraps, and smoothies.

Green Briar (Smilax bona-nox)

This plant is also known as Cat briar, and Blaspheme Vine

Ask me how I know about the last one! Off-trail hiking or foraging can be treacherous if you stumble into this thorny tangle! Extricating oneself can be a painful process. But wait! It has redeeming qualities which we shall discuss. If discovered early in the year, the young tendrils and leaves are quite tender and tasty as a steamed green or added to any cooked dish you choose. Interestingly, Greenbrier is an ingredient of the historical sarsaparilla beverage! Here's a recipe for Greenbrier casserole!

Greenbrier Casserole

INGREDIENTS

Greenbrier shoots
Melted butter,
Sliced boiled eggs,
6 tablespoons flour
6 tablespoons melted butter.
2 cups milk
½ teaspoon salt
½ teaspoon pepper
1/8 teaspoon nutmeg
1 cup grated cheddar cheese.

INSTRUCTIONS

Boil greenbrier shoots for a few minutes, drain, and coat with melted butter. Layer into a greased casserole dish, then top with a layer of sliced boiled eggs, another greenbrier layer, egg layer, etc., ending with a greenbrier layer. Make a sauce of 6 tablespoons melted butter, blend in 6 tablespoons flour, whisk in 2 cups hot milk, ½ teaspoon salt, ½ teaspoon pepper, ⅛ teaspoon nutmeg. Add 1 cup grated cheddar cheese and pour over your casserole. 350 degrees, 30 minutes. Good heavenly days!

Henbit (Lamium amplexicaule)

This one's an early riser, even springing up in the winter months. If given the go-ahead, it will quickly supply an abundance of tasty, tipped foliage and beautiful purple flowers. It's a bit hairy to my taste, but by cooking in a spare amount of water, adding a dab of butter, perhaps some spring onions.... top with a bit of sour cream, and you've got something! It's quite palatable and extremely nutritious, low in calories, and rich in antioxidants and minerals.

Dead Nettle (Lamium purpureum)

Dead nettle is found in late winter and early spring. It's sometimes called by several names like red nettle or purple nettle. You'll notice the pretty purplish red terminal leaves and pink flowers. It's called dead nettle, not because it is dead, but because it doesn't have the "sting" of the stinging nettle. You'll quickly learn to know the difference!

This close relative of henbit is a native to the Ozarks and grows in planting beds as a weed. Despite its common appearance, dead nettle is a valuable wild edible and medicinal plant. It's a great source of vitamins C, A, and K, as well as iron, fiber, and bioflavonoids.

The whole plant has a mildly sweet flavor, and the young tender leaves have a light peppery taste when eaten raw. They are a fantastic addition to any salad. Just like its stinging sister, dead nettle is also a substitute for greens like spinach, kale, and lettuce. You can also blend them with other greens (once you know you don't have an allergy to one of them, of course) and lemon juice for a delicious green smoothie.

Their leaves can also be cooked as a potherb. Much like any other greens, these leaves will taste great when stir-fried. They will also be a fantastic addition to soups and stews. If you want something different, try dipping them in a tempura batter and deep-fry them for a delicious and crunchy snack.

Tempura Batter

INGREDIENTS

1 ½ cup cornstarch
¾ teaspoon salt
¾ cup COLD water
1 egg
Peanut or vegetable oil for frying

INSTRUCTIONS

Blend all but the oil together with a whisk, don't over-mix. Dip the individual leaves into the batter and drop carefully one by one into the hot frying oil, keeping each separate. Don't overcrowd. Flip when golden brown, watch carefully, and remove to drain on paper towels, salt a bit and enjoy (once, they've cooled down).

Lady's Thumb and Knotweed (Persicaria) many varieties, Smartweed (Persicaria amphibia-formerly Polygonum amphibium)

This common as-all-get-out vegetable (yes, a vegetable!) is something I thought of as a consequence of setting out hay rings and bales in our pastures all winter. The resulting bald spot each spring seemed to be the ideal growing spot for this little booger!

Also known as Smartweed, its pink or white flowers are attractive, but our cows rarely graze on it. I now know why. Gathering the young leaves in the spring yields a tasty addition to welcome early salads and is also a wonderful peppery potherb. I've found the pink flowering variety is less peppery, and the white ones are more robust. Your choice. Simply boil for 5-10 minutes until tender as you would spinach and use accordingly in any recipe calling for greens. Lasagna, quiche, soups, you get the idea! Don't overlook another use: dried leaves of the white flowering variety can be crumbled in any recipe calling for pepper.

Lamb's Quarters (Chenopodium album)

When wild edible references state this "weed" is found state-wide, I'd say nationwide is more accurate. I'd wager there isn't a state where it is NOT found growing freely. Great news! Wherever you may roam, you can count on having access to this mild, nutritious green.

Even after you've done fall cleanup in your yard or garden, its dormant seeds will probably sprout in the disturbed soil and supply a ratoon harvest without any effort on your part. Raw in a salad, simmered in soups and stews, simply boiled like spinach, all good. Just be aware that lamb's quarters are high in oxalic acid so should be eaten sparingly by folks sensitive to developing kidney stones and related ailments.

Live Forever, Stone Crop (Sedum thartii)

You'll recognize this as a common landscape or home foundation "shrub". Being a perennial, it dies back to the ground in winter months here in the Ozarks but sprouts again in early spring, the best time to harvest some young succulent leaves for some good eating. Add the very young leaves to an early foraged green salad or prepare as follows.

Gather the leaves in mid-summer and boil until tender. Then coat with butter for a nice tasty cooked green.

Chunky Salad

In late spring, harvest a number of foraged salad makings can be combined to make a delicious salad bowl. Purslane, stonecrop leaves, young wild grape tendrils, some violet flowers for color, and chunky feta cheese. Keep in mind, ratios are up to the cook, however stone crop is best kept to a minimum, due to its comparatively strong flavor.

Wild Mustard (Brassica nigra)

The wild mustard common to the Ozarks is known as commonly known as winter cress or yellow rocket. This leafy, relative of the cabbage is a many-branched plant that grows to 2 feet tall. You'll find it in many gardens and fields and are recognized by their many yellow flowers that bloom from April–June. The fruit is a long seedpod that forms at the bottom of the cluster as new flowers open at the tips of the flower stalks.

As you take a country drive in late spring, you've probably noticed little lovely yellow flowers in road ditches and fields, it's probably field mustard. Look closely at how similar plant parts of this weed resembles the garden varieties-flowers like broccoli, leaves like kale, stems like kohlrabi. That's because they're family!

It might interest you to know this important food family contains 4,064 species. The vast majority have been selectively bred over time to produce such familiar varieties as broccoli cabbage, kale, cauliflower, and so many more. It's nice to know that with all the common field mustard that we have here, all parts are edible.

These mustard greens can be eaten in many ways. Eat them raw as part of a mixed spring green salad. You can make a creamy mustard green sauce to drizzle over potatoes or chicken. Use it in Indian cooking and try adding it to Asian stir fry! It's international Ozarks at its best!

You can also preserve it for later by blanching it (steam it to lightly wilt it) and freezing the amount you are likely to use at a time. Dry it for making a green powder to add to soups, sauces, or smoothies.

Flowery Mustard

Mustard flowers have a pungent mustard taste, so only a small amount is needed This mustard is strong and only requires a small amount to flavor your dish. Try it!

INGREDIENTS

1 cup fresh mustard flowers
½ cup of white wine vinegar or apple cider vinegar
1 garlic clove
1 teaspoon salt
Spices to taste (choose from rosemary, oregano, thyme, basil, sage)

INSTRUCTIONS

Simply grind this up with a mortar and pestle, refrigerate, and enjoy. I like to keep it sealed up in a pretty, little Dijon jar, recycled, of course

***

Flavorsome Skillet

Sauté the wild mustard greens alone or include them in scrambled eggs, add it to soups and salads. Explore the possibilities.

Stinging Nettle (Laportea canadensis)

Stinging nettle is not native but naturalized to the Ozarks. Because of its many health benefits and versatility, the plant traveled with explorers throughout the world and now grows abundantly in the Ozarks.

This plant is called "stinging" for a reason! On the leaf surface are tiny hairs that can cause an itchy, burning rash when touched that may last half a day. Best to use gloves when gathering these!

Clean this plant before you cook it. You don't want to ingest the stinging hairs. Wash it well while wearing gloves to break up the needles or cook it down so they melt away.

Anything you can do with spinach you can do with stinging nettle, and more. Cook it down like a leafy green and add to soup and creamy risotto, layer it into lasagna, and bake into egg dishes. Blend it with yogurt, honey, and fruit like you would spinach or kale for an extra-nutritious smoothie. However, remember that if you want to use it raw, first crush the hollow "needles" flat using the blunt end of a knife or pressing down with a rolling pin. Be sure to wear gloves when doing this so you don't get stung. Blanching the leaves in boiling water will also remove the stinging trichomes.

Nettle roots can be dug up and brought in the late fall and kept during the winter to be forced or grown inside by placing it in moist sand in the basement and waiting for it to send up its white stalk. Whether eaten raw or cooked into any vegetable or meat stew, these young shoots and their leaves are both very good and nutritious.

Store about a dozen plants per person to have plenty to last through the winter.

Remember to always wear gloves when handling stinging nettle!

Nettle Pudding

INGREDIENTS

Heaping cup of nettle greens,
One large, chopped onion (or half cup wild garlic greens and bulbs),
1 ½ cups of ground venison or ground beef,

3 slices of bacon chopped,
1/8 teaspoon salt,
1/8 teaspoon sage,

INSTRUCTIONS

Put all ingredients into a clean white cheese cloth and boil for about an hour in a large kettle. Serve with milk gravy and butter.

Perilla Mint (perilla frutescens)

This common Ozark plant is wild Shiso! Are you familiar with the cultivated Asian variety? Other common names are beefsteak mint or wild basil. Take a nibble of a leaf and you'll have a taste that's minty, cinnamon-y, licorice-y. Experiment and add a little to rice or pasta, and the tender flower buds can be battered and fried. While it's toxic to cattle (they usually shun it unless there is little else to pick from) human folks have eaten and enjoyed it for centuries. It's easy to pick out in pastures, shady waste places, and fence rows due to the tell-tale square mint stalk, purple undersides of the leaves, tall seed stalk, and spicy aroma when crushed.

Plantain (Plantago sp.)

When I was a kid, we used to call the broadleaf plantain "bunny weed." The reason we called it that was because our pet rabbits loved the stuff. Though dismissed as a pervasive garden weed pest because it grows everywhere from the area between the bricks in a sidewalk to shallow fields, plantain is not only edible and readily, but it has been used for centuries in traditional medicine.

Several other types exist within the same family. The variety of plantains that are common in the Ozarks includes narrow-leaf plantain (Plantago lanceolata), blackseed plantain (Plantago rugelii), blond plantain (Plantago ovata), (a common source of psyllium) bracted plantain (Plantago aristata), wooly plantain (Plantago patagonica), and even the Heart-leaved Plantain (Plantago chordata).

Heart-leaved plantain (Plantago chordata) was once common throughout the eastern United States and this plant survives only in a small handful of sites outside the Ozarks. The Ozarks are its last stronghold. Siltation, pollution, and other water quality degradation of previously clear, gravel bottom streams caused this plant to disappear from much of its former range. However, it can be found in small gravel creeks throughout the Ozarks region.

The leaves of all plantains are edible and highly nutritious. They have vitamins A, D, and K as well as the minerals iron and magnesium. You want to eat only the young leaves because older leaves are so tough that they can be used as a string for fishing lines or used to twist into a rope.

Young leaves can be sautéed, stir-fried, or steamed. Add them to dishes just like other greens or use the tenderest young leaves as salad greens. Plantain can be dried, stored, and then be crumbled to sprinkle into soups for a winter nutritional boost.

Plantain Soup

(A fantastic way to use leftovers!)

INGREDIENTS

2 cups plantain leaves cut into julienne strips ¼ inch wide
4 cups turkey, chicken, or beef broth

INSTRUCTIONS

Boil for four minutes.

To create a more substantial soup add other cooked ingredients like:

Cooked noodles

Rice

Other vegetables

Chunks of meat like chicken, beef, or venison.

Add noodles, meat, and/or vegetables to the pot and partially cook add the plantain during the last four minutes of cooking.

***

Plantain 'Goma Ae'

INGREDIENTS

2 cups plantain leaves

2 tablespoons sesame seed oil

2 tablespoons soy sauce

Sesame seeds

INSTRUCTIONS

Take two cups of plantain leaves and boil them in water for 4 minutes. Shock the leaves in ice water and then squeeze from them as much water as you can.

Mix 2 tablespoons of *sesame seed oil* with 2 tablespoons of *soy sauce* and toss the leaves in the sauce.

Form the leaves into cubes with your fingers. You should get about 4 cubes in total from 2 cups of leaves.

Drizzle any remaining sauce over each and sprinkle with sesame seeds. This is especially good with rice and other Asian dishes.

Poke Sallet or Poke Weed (Phytolacca americana)

Caution: *Because of its poisonous reputation, many folks are afraid to eat poke. If you don't follow the rules for cooking it, poke could kill you or make you so sick you would wish you were dead. If eaten, those pretty, dark purple berries growing on this tall weed with red stems will kill you! The entire raw plant is highly toxic and filled with several different active compounds.*

Newly emerged poke sallet greens, however, are delicious and nutritious depending on how you eat them. Other stages of growth and other parts of the plant can be poisonous and deadly. As with everything else, do your research before eating poke. Always keep children and pets away from any parts of raw pokeweed.

Poke sallet is a weed that goes by several different names including poke salad, Polk weed, Virginia poke, or poke bush.

Many Ozarks folk eat cooked poke sallet with eggs every spring. Backyard chicken flocks produce lots of eggs here in the Ozarks when Poke is in season, so this makes a good combination.

Poke plants have light rose-tinted young stems, and the leaves have smoother edges than other greens. Pick Poke at the right time of year. The best time to gather poke is when it first emerges as sprouts a green in the spring.

Not only do you need to pick poke when they haven't developed more than just as greens, but poke also needs to be prepared properly before consuming. Basic and simple but important steps for safely preparing poke include cutting, deveining, boiling, straining, cooking in fresh water, straining it again, and cooking it in another pan of fresh water before adding the poke as a delicious ingredient to recipes that include it. Always go through all these steps before consuming because poke cannot *safely* be eaten raw. You might be told "Granny and Grandpa ate the berries all the time! And they died of natural causes!" Just nod and say "No doubt, no doubt. My condolences." Remember, all parts are poisonous raw.

If you want to freeze some for a later date, don't leave the poke raw but put them through the cooking process shared in the paragraph above before putting them into freezer bags or containers.

When making fried poke and eggs, fry the previously prepared poke with eggs in pork back fat.

If you're not into eating eggs, poke, like many other greens, can be cooked with onions and bacon grease. Once the poke is wilted, add some crunch by sprinkling crumbled bacon on top.

You can also use it in other ways like poke and artichoke dip, poke and cream sauce over pasta, poke quiche, poke in smoked chicken chili, or poke green pasta. Just remember to always cook it!

Common Purslane (Portulaca oleracea)

This humble little *superfood* has the highest level of plant-based omega-3 fatty acids, in addition to so many vitamins and minerals. Your own research can supply many interesting recipes, and it's so easy to include them on your menu in many ways. Leaves, stems and seeds are all very edible and tasty, having a slightly citrusy flavor. You've probably seen it almost everywhere in disturbed soil, garden spots, and flower beds. Maybe, even growing through cracks in the sidewalk(next to the plantain)! When you gather it, just make sure your harvest area is a clean environment, and then you'll feel confident eating it raw or cooked as an addition to soups, stews, and stir-fries.

Redbud (Cercis canadensis)

The striking purple Redbud blossoms have always been such a welcome sight each spring following our blustery Ozarks winter. In March and April, the hills and hollers seem to come alive with Redbud blossoms, and the pollinators happily take advantage of the nectar flow.

Once you're able to gather a fistful of blossoms, add as many of the clean blossoms as you like to your pancake batter. Simply use your favorite pancake mix or recipe. Fritters are another way to enjoy them.

Redbud Pancakes

INGREDIENTS

As many clean red bud blossoms as you wish to gather
1 Teaspoon Baking Powder
½ teaspoon salt
1 cup flour
Mix dry ingredients and set aside.
In another bowl, mix wet ingredients,
1 farm egg
¼ cup milk
¼ cup cooking oil

INSTRUCTIONS

Mix dry and wet ingredients together, and add as many clean redbud blossoms as you wish to gather.

Drop and fry the batter in one inch of hot oil in a skillet until your pancakes are golden brown. Drain pancakes on paper towels. Drizzle with orange juice and dust with powdered sugar. Now that's some larruping eating!

Reindeer Lichen (Cladonia rangiferina)

Here on our farm in south central Missouri, there is a dense thicket of cedar covering an otherwise erodible rocky slope. It's a perfect patch of cover for the many deer and turkeys that inhabit our place. Along the old logging road that winds through, I've found a wonderful patch of reindeer lichen, and have very carefully gathered just enough to use, but not eradicate the entire area. This lichen can be gathered year-round and is brittle and dry in summer, spongy and wet when rain graces the area. Here are just a few ways to use this edible, usually ground and used as an addition to flour in many favorite recipes.

Lift the lichen easily off the ground and cut away the soil from the bottom of this low-growing plant. Rinse and place in a warm area or dehydrator to dry thoroughly, and crush to a coarse powder for storage. This "flour" can easily be substituted for half of the flour in any recipe, and here's one to get you started. You won't be disappointed!

Reindeer Lichen Biscuits

INGREDIENTS

4 tablespoons unsalted butter
1 ¼ cup all-purpose flour
¼ cup crushed reindeer lichen
3 teaspoons baking powder,
¼ teaspoon salt
¾ cup milk

INSTRUCTIONS

Cut 4 tablespoons of unsalted butter into 1 ¼ cup all-purpose flour, ¼ cup dried, crushed reindeer lichen, 3 teaspoons baking powder, and 1/4 teaspoon salt. Add 3/4 cup milk and mix with a fork, just until the dough holds together. Roll or pat out on a floured board and cut with a round biscuit cutter. (You do have one, right?) Or alternately into 3" finger-like strips. Bake at 450 degrees for 12-15 minutes. Butter? Honey? Yes, please!

Sassafras (sassafras albidum)

We won't entertain using the root in tea, as there is some controversy over whether it is toxic to the liver. So just be your own judge, but here's an interesting way to enjoy this plant's flavor in recipes.

Filé Powder

Gather a fistful of young sassafras leaves,
De-vein and wash, pat dry
Lay the leaves in one layer on dehydrator screens and dry at about 95 degrees, if your unit has a fan, that's ideal.
Dry until crisp and immediately rub through a fine sieve or food processor to create a fine powder.
Use this to thicken Gumbo or any stew. Filé is more than a thickener; it also imparts an earthy flavor and has a fruity aroma similar to coriander seeds.
Thanks go to my Ozark neighbor, Sharon Hudson, originally from La Fayette Louisiana, she's developed her own Ozarks Style family recipe for File Gumbo. She shares it with us.

Ozark Style Gumbo

First, make the roux.

INSTRUCTIONS

1 cup flour 3/4 cup vegetable oil of choice. (Not olive oil)
In a large heavy-bottomed "Gumbo Pot" over medium-high heat, constantly stir flour and oil with a spatula-type flat-edged wooden spoon until dark brown. Do not leave it unattended. (This wooden utensil is very important. Miss Sharon's

is literally black from being used exclusively for gumbo!) Once dark brown, set the roux aside to cool. It will be added later.

It's useful to have prepared the following the day before, but not essential:

1 Rotisserie chicken, boiled, cooled, deboned, and chopped.

To the broth thus prepared, add the Cajun's "Holy Trinity" of

1 large, chopped onion,

1 large, chopped bell pepper,

4 stocks of chopped celery,

Add a few cloves of chopped garlic, chopped green onions if you like.

2 cups chunked sausages (Andouille is traditional, but the smoked polish is also a possibility)

Every "good gumbo" has lots of seasoning! Examples include the following seasonings.

Tony's Creole Seasoning,

 Mrs. Dash's,

Salt & pepper to taste,

and of course,

2-3 tablespoons file powder

Bring to a boil and slowly stir in the cooled roux.

Pour this glorious creamy creation onto a bowl of cooked rice. This mixture will coat the rice and leave your tongue slappin' your forehead with deliciousness.

Spiderwort (Tradescantia virginiana ohiensis)

As a good potherb alone or mixed with other foraged greens, it doesn't need a long cooking time.

The fresh deep blue flowers can be candied or added to salads as a beautiful spring addition.

Violet, common blue (Viola sororia)

Where shall we start? This lovely "field pansy" is not only beautiful in the spring, but one of the most nutritious natives in the Ozarks. The tender leaves can have as much as double the amount of vitamin C as citrus, per weight, and easily double the amount of vitamin A as spinach. Any of the many colors of blooms are edible, and leaves can be stir-fried or steamed and used in cooked dishes. Introduce the children in your life to this sweet little blossom, have them pick a handful to add to the family salad and they'll happily learn to eat their veggies with gusto.

Watercress (Nasturtium officinale -syn. Rorippa nasturtium-aquaticum)

Watercress is a salad and pot herb that has a "newer botanical classification", but we digress. This perennial plant grows in our fine, clear-running streams and rivers in abundance.

It can be tossed fresh into any salad or soup and as a pungent garnish for meat or fish.

Or:

Fry two strips of bacon. Crumble them over a bowl of clean, washed watercress leaves and wilt them by bringing to a boil equal amounts of bacon grease (Granny's secret ingredient) water, and vinegar. Add 1 tablespoon of sugar to this boiling mix along with a pinch of salt. Pour immediately over your greens, stir up a bit, and enjoy.

~ 3 ~

OZARK FORAGEABLE FRUITS

Public domain clipart

Autumn Olive (Elaeagnus umbellata)

Caution: *Autumn olive is an aggressively invasive hedgerow plant and should not be allowed to spread willy-nilly. Do be aware that it is a suckering bush and is also spread by birds and mammals. The seeds survive their digestive tract, so if you plant one, you'll have one thousand in a few years.*

You would think by the name "autumn olive" this plant should be considered a vegetable. However, it is included here in fruits because of its sweetness and because autumn olive is a type of berry and is used like one.

In addition to autumn olive, this plant goes by several different aliases like autumn berry, Japanese silverberry, Umbellata oleaster, autumn Elaeagnus, or spreading oleaster.

Autumn olive was brought to the Ozarks in the 1830s and was commonly planted for wildlife food, shelter belts, erosion control, wasteland reclamation, wildlife habitat, and in gardens as an ornamental. Don't confuse Autumn olive with Russian olive. These medium-sized deciduous invasive bushes from Asia can grow up to sixteen feet tall.

They are not hard to identify if you know what to look for. Their shrubs produce alternate green leaves that are oval-shaped with finely pointed tips. The leaves are darker green on top with beautiful silvery undersides. They appear from March through April depending on location.

One plus about these shrubs is that the flowers are an important source of nectar for pollinators such as bees and other insects.

Autumn olive's abundant fruits are silvery with brown scales when young and ripen to a deep red with silvery or brown speckles in September and October. They have the shape of very tiny olives, and their leaves resemble that of olive tree leaves. The delicious fruits are eaten by a variety of birds, insects, and mammals (me included).

Every autumn olive berry has a seed with a pointed end and lines running along its length. Autumn Olive is shade intolerant and prefers dry sites. You will not find them in wet areas or dense forests. Instead, they are found in open woods, along forest edges, roadsides, sand dunes, and other disturbed areas. I have several growing around the edge of my yard and beside the garden shed under our maple tree.

Their red color is not a sufficient indicator of ripeness. If you are in doubt, you can tell by feel and by taste. Autumn olive berries have a pleasant sour tanginess when fully ripe, but underripe ones are unpleasantly astringent and unpalatable. When ready for harvest, the fruit should be soft and plump. The best way to determine ripeness is to know when they are likely to ripen in your area. Autumn olive berries are usually ready in the Ozarks from late summer through the autumn months.

To collect their berries, hold a large bowl or container under a branch laden with berries, and gently rub your other hand down the branch. If the berries are ripe, they will fall off easily into your container. If not, they'll cling to the branch. You can come back in a day or two to get the rest.

Autumn olive berries are high in vitamins A, C, and E, and minerals like phosphorous, magnesium, calcium, and potassium. They also contain iron as well as essential fatty acids, and bioflavonoids, and are rich in ascorbic acid. They have seventeen times the lycopene of ripe tomatoes.

The fruit and seeds are edible and can be used in jam, jellies, and preserves as well as eaten raw. The leaves can be used in tea. Once you have some autumn berries, they can be eaten fresh, pureed, frozen, made into jam or sauces, or fermented into wine.

The berries can be dried and stored to use in fruity herbal teas or tisanes. The flowers can also be used in herbal teas along with the leaves.

Here's a recipe that the kids in your family will really love!

Autumn Olive Berry Fruit Leather

INGREDIENTS

8-10 cups of ripe autumn olive berries
Four to eight ounces of water
Honey to taste

INSTRUCTIONS

Add berries and water to a large pot on the stove. Heat the pot over high heat, and bring the liquid to a simmer, while stirring and mashing the berries. Reduce heat on low and simmer until most berries have burst. This should take about 10 minutes.

Remove seeds and stems from the liquid by pushing the pulp through a fine mesh sieve or a food mill.

Add honey to taste as a sweetener if desired.

IN THE DEHYDRATOR

Lightly coat 2 fruit roll sheets or parchment paper with vegetable oil. Thinly spread berry mixture over sheets and place in dehydrator tray. Set dehydrator to 135-140 degrees F and dry for 10 hours, or until fruit is no longer sticky. Your kids will love it!

Blackberry (Rubus spp.)

Picking Blackberries

Here in the Ozarks, blackberry season occurs during the second half of June and the first half of July. Blackberry picking can be quite challenging, and beginners have no idea what they are getting themselves into when they go blackberry picking. The first thing they don't realize is how scorching hot it gets in late June and into July, so they soon learn it's best to choose the time when the heat isn't unbearable. Some people like to go blackberry picking in the evening, but I prefer to gather the berries in the early morning around 6 am.

Next, it's important to dress for the event. When I dress for blackberry picking, I wear my tall rubber boots so that I protect my feet and lower legs from getting chiggers, touching poison ivy, and potentially surprising a copperhead that is sleeping in the shade of the berry briars. Next, I wear a good pair of cotton socks to absorb the sweat that I know will accumulate inside the boot and put on a good thick pair of jeans to protect my legs from the briars. I wear a long-sleeved shirt for the same reason. A good hat to protect my face from the sun finishes my ensemble.

To keep my hands free to pick the berries, I make a bucket to carry the berries. I take a well-rinsed recycled plastic milk jug and cut out the top so that there's a hole big enough to accept the berries, but I leave the handle intact. I lace the handle through a belt and secure the belt around my waist. This allows me to have hands-free picking. I have done this for years to prevent berries from accidentally getting spilled when I am reaching for one of those juicy fruits.

Once I have filled the jug, I am ready to take the bucket into the house for processing.

At the house, before taking care of the berries, I take care of my own needs. As I enter the house I remove the extra warm clothes, not just because they are extra warm, but also because there could be unwelcome guests riding along. Yes, I am speaking about ticks. I remove the clothes at the door and immediately throw them into the washing machine and turn on the machine. In addition, I take a shower and have my husband check me for ticks. I have several friends who have tick-borne diseases so ridding myself of these insects is a very effective way to avoid diseases from these pests. Once I am clean and dressed in cooler clothes, it is time to take care of the blackberries.

To take care of the blackberries, I ensure that the blackberries are clean and bug-free. We're not the only ones who like blackberries! To wash the berries, I put them into a pan of cold water and pull the berries out of the water a handful at a time into a strainer to rid them of the excess water. While pulling them out, I inspect them for leaves or worms that may have been eating them. In addition, I remove any stems that stay attached to the berries. Once the berries are done, I can either put them in plastic bags and put them in the freezer, or I can process them further if I have the time.

Here are a couple of my favorite recipes using blackberries.

What is a Blackberry Cobbler?

What's the difference between blackberry cobbler and blackberry pie? According to several sites that I found online, a cobbler has one top crust, and a pie has a bottom crust and a top crust. Also, a cobbler is only fruit, and pies can be fruit, meat, or vegetable. However, here in the Ozarks, many of us call any berry pie that has a bottom or top crust a cobbler. Don't try to change us. That's just the way we call it! I have been told by many residents who have lived in the Ozarks all their lives that a blackberry cobbler is a two-crust pie. Period.

Now, let me show you how I make blackberry cobbler. The first step in preparing the berries for the cobbler is to wash them as explained previously. If bought from the grocery store or farmers' market, a quick rinse is about all I would need to do. When using the blackberries that I packaged and put in the freezer, I can skip this step altogether. When I feel that I have cleaned out all the debris, pour the blackberries into a colander to drain all the excess water.

Now that you've paid your dues to collect a gallon or two let's make a blackberry cobbler!

Blackberry Cobbler

Preheat oven to 425 degrees Fahrenheit and gather ingredients for blackberry filling.

INGREDIENTS

2 quarts of blackberries
1 cup sugar
½ teaspoon cinnamon
2 tablespoons cornstarch (or all-purpose flour)

INSTRUCTIONS

Mix the ingredients and set aside while you make the pie dough. No cooking is necessary at this point. All the cooking happens in the baking pan.

Two-Crust Pie Dough

INGREDIENTS

2 cups white flour (sifted)
1 teaspoon salt
2/3 cup shortening or lard (Granny's secret: lard makes flakier pie crust)
4 tablespoons water, ice cold
1 tablespoon butter

INSTRUCTIONS

Mix flour and salt, then cut in the shortening or lard. For best results, make sure that you have mixed the flour, salt, and shortening thoroughly so that you won't have to mix as much after you add the water. Finally add ice-cold water, the colder the water, the better your crust will be. Gather dough together and press it into a ball.

Divide the pastry dough in half. Round up the first half onto a lightly floured board covered with wax paper. Lightly dust dough with flour

Flatten with hand, and roll out to not quite 1/2 inch thick. Work quickly and roll lightly. Do not add extra flour or you will get tougher pastry dough. If it breaks apart, pinch the broken edges together.

Roll out the pastry to about one inch larger around than the pan you are using. Fold the pastry along with the wax paper in half and quickly move the dough to the pan. Unfold the pastry and remove the wax paper. Fit pastry around the side of a 9x9 inch pan (square or round, doesn't matter). If the dough breaks, Pat broken edges with water and pinch the dough into place.

Pour berry mixture into pan.

Dot (distribute tiny pieces) of butter over the top of the filling. Moisten the edges of the crust with water.

Roll out the top crust of the pastry the same way that you rolled the bottom crust. Fold in half. Moisten the lower pie crust edges with water and lay evenly over the top crust over the filling. Unfold. Press down the edges of the top onto the edges of the bottom crust.

Cut away excess dough, sprinkle the top of the cobbler with cinnamon sugar.

Place the pan on a cookie sheet and the cobbler into a preheated oven. Bake for 45 minutes or until the crust is nicely browned and juice begins to bubble through the slits in the crust.

Makes 9 servings. Best served warm, not hot, and with ice cream or whipped topping.

(This pie crust recipe can be used for other pies too like the Black Walnut Pie on pages 92-93,)

Black Raspberry (Rubus occidentalis)

As a transplant to the Missouri Ozarks myself nearly 40 years ago, I was immediately delighted to see so many of the same foraged plants I came to know in the foothills of central California. One that was new to me, however, came as a "welcome to the area" gift from my new neighbor, herself a native of our community. She brought me a few "starts" of the naturalized black raspberry bush that is found everywhere right out there in the woods.

The story goes that the original plants came west with some of the thrifty Scotch-Irish families who settled many of our Ozark counties. They came and stayed, as did their raspberries. Once you spy the purplish spiny canes resembling blackberries in the wild, they will easily transplant back to your yard and will supply a delectable addition to your forage foods. Just remember they prefer a semi-shady spot, for, after all, they're found in the understory of those woods.

Black Raspberry Jelly

The number one best way to enjoy them is right off the bush in June and July. Alternatively, you can make jelly.

INSTRUCTIONS

Cover rinsed berries with water and simmer for 10-15 minutes. Drain off most of the liquid for jelly.

Extract liquid from cooked berries as per above

One cup of sugar per cup of raspberry juice.

For each of these small batches, use one package of Sure Jell.

Boil this all together in a large pan, for the foam will rise.

Follow any approved recipe for processing, I would suggest going with half-pint jelly jars to portion out through the winter months.

This jelly is perfect with those reindeer lichen biscuits from the previous recipe!

Crab Apple (Malus coronaria)

Wild apples, including crabapples, are the tree from which all cultivated varieties of apple (Malus domestica) were developed. Unlike cultivars, wild apples always grow from seed and each one is genetically unique, potentially hardier, and better adapted to local conditions than cultivars.

After the flowers have been pollinated, small apples will appear, and many will drop earlier in the season. Don't worry about this phenomenon. It's normal and you can use these small bitter-sour tiny apples to make your own pectin.

Since moving here to the Ozarks, I discovered that pectin is not such a mysterious substance as I thought it was. Pectin is found in green apples. Pectin made from apples can be added to fruits that do not normally jell on their own. Fruit low in pectin, including apricots, blueberries, cherries, elderberries, peaches, pears, pineapple, raspberries, and strawberries will not gel without adding a thickener such as pectin.

Homemade Pectin (from early drop apples) Recipe!

I use any early drop from any form of apple including crabapple. I like using those unripe, early falls even though they produce cloudier pectin. I like the fact that I have a constructive use for these immature apples and crabapples. (After I have picked up the apples for pectin, I allow the chickens to clean up the remaining early-drop apples.) If I do not have enough time to make a batch of pectin when the apples are first available, I can freeze the apples in the freezer until I am ready to make my pectin. I just wash them and put them into a container and freeze them. It's as simple as that! If I do not have enough early fall apples, I have added just ripe, or slightly under-ripe apples for pectin making. However, you cannot make pectin using overly ripe apples.

Homemade Apple Pectin Recipe

INGREDIENTS

2 lbs. of early fall apples or slightly under-ripe apple parts (peelings, cores, pulp, or whole apples)
4 cups of water

INSTRUCTIONS

1. In the pot, I put the apples with just enough water to cover all the pieces. I bring the apples and water to a boil. I turn my burner down to simmer and simmer it for about an hour.
2. I place my strainer over the plastic container and then lay the cheesecloth over the strainer. I pour the cooked apples and water into the cheesecloth. I don't squeeze the bag because squeezing the bag will create cloudy pectin. Instead, I leave this to drain overnight so that I will get the lion's share of the liquid from my fruit before continuing with the next step.
3. In the morning I discard the apples either to the compost or to feed my chickens (they love me for it!) I pour the liquid drained from the apples back into a saucepan and boil for fifteen more minutes. I now have my homemade pectin. If I cannot use it right away, sometimes freeze it or can it for later use.

Getting the pectin to work is not an exact science. Because each apple's content of pectin, sugar, and acids varies, each batch of pectin will be slightly different. I sometimes need to adjust the amount of pectin used and how long I need to cook the jelly for best results. I test my pectin to give me an idea of my homemade pectin's level of effectiveness and test my finished batch of jelly or jam before canning it up.

To test my homemade pectin, I put one tablespoon of rubbing alcohol and one teaspoon of the homemade pectin into a container and stir. My pectin should form a glob at the top of the alcohol. I throw the alcohol and pectin mixture away and I boil a batch of pectin a little longer.

The pectin produced is not the same as commercial pectin. The pectin I have created requires a little bit more flexibility.

For each cup of fruit juice (or fruit pulp) used, I use one cup of homemade pectin and one and one-half cups of sugar. I place fruit or juice and pectin into a saucepan and bring to a boil. I add sugar and return it to a boil. I then boil the mixture for one minute.

I make sure that my jam or jelly sets up by properly checking it before spooning it into jars. I remove a teaspoon of my cooked jelly and hold the spoon over an ice cube to cool. When the cooled jelly sets up and thickens, my jelly or jam is ready. If not, I add another cup of sugar, two ounces of lemon juice (1/4 cup), and more of the homemade pectin. I boil the mixture for another minute and check again.

I could freeze any excess homemade pectin. I leave a one-inch of headspace for expansion. I, however, prefer to can it if I am not using my homemade pectin right away this way I have pectin available when early drop apples aren't available. To can apple pectin, I heat it to boiling, pour it into sterilized canning jars, and seal it. I use the boiling-water bath method for ten minutes to preserve my pectin, which is the same way and length of time that my county extension office recommends for canning apple juice.

Now that you know how to make your own pectin from those little green apples that you probably would have just let go to waste, you'll want to make all sorts of jellies and jams from all kinds of fruits available to you.

Common Elderberries (Sambucus canadensis),

Caution: *Many parts of elderberry plants are poisonous. Only eat the berries and never eat them raw. See below for how to process berries.*

The common names for elderberries include European elder, black elder, elderberry, and elderflower.

I was first introduced to elderberries as a child. My mother had a bush at the corner of the house that produced an abundance of bluish-black fruit that grew in bunches. The berries themselves are quite bitter, so they are rarely eaten alone. She used elderberries to make blackberry elderberry or apple elderberry pies.

During the past few years, my husband and I have been going out along the roadside, picking elderberries to make elderberry jelly or elderberry syrup. One of my former neighbors uses elderberries to make wine.

Remove all stems, stem pieces, and unripe berries from your elderberries before storing them. Elderberries will keep whole in the freezer. They can also be dried in a food dehydrator. Before using it, you must always cook your elderberries.

Mash elderberries gently to release the juice when preparing the berries for juicing. Cover the berries with water and boil until the berries become grayish. Strain out the berries and use the juice for making jellies and syrups.

Elderberry Syrup from Dried Berries

INGREDIENTS

3½ cups water
⅔ cup dried elderberries (or 1 1/3 cups fresh or frozen)
2 tablespoon ginger (grated)

1 tsp cinnamon
½ tsp ground cloves
1 cup raw honey from a local source

INSTRUCTIONS

Pour the water into a saucepan and add the elderberries, ginger, cinnamon, and cloves.

Bring to a boil and then uncover and reduce to a simmer for about 30 to 45 minutes until the liquid has reduced by almost half.

Remove from heat. When cool enough to handle, mash the berries carefully with a spoon or other flat utensil. (Can blend in blender.)

Pour through a strainer and into a glass jar or bowl. Discard the berries.

Add the cup of honey and stir well.

Pour the syrup into a mason jar or glass bottle.

Wild Grape (Vitus spp.)

There are eight varieties of wild grapes in the Ozarks. Many Ozarkians call them "Possum Grapes,"

Vitis varieties have several things in common. These grapes are native or naturalized in the Ozarks and all have edible fruits. The plant's perennial woody vines typically climb into trees with tendrils. These tendrils are positioned opposite to leaves and are often branched and have no thorns or spines.

Stems are often swollen at the nodes; with a brown pith, or interior, (easiest to see on branches less than ½ inch in diameter) and usually seen on older branches; the bark usually shredding.

The fruits are globe-shaped berries, often blue-black, with a white waxy coating. Seeds 1–4 per fruit, pear-shaped.

These grapes are used in any way that grapes have been used. They are sometimes used to make jelly or wine and are even eaten fresh.

The leaves can also be used in making brine pickles. To use in making pickles, layer vegetables to be pickled, grape leaves, and pickling salt into a food-grade bucket or crock. The salt will cause the vegetables to release their water. Once the bucket is full, you should have plenty of liquid so that you can weigh the vegetables down until they are covered with water by using a plate and a brick that has been scrubbed clean. Put these in a cool location of about 65 degrees Fahrenheit for ten days or longer. The longer you leave the pickles in the brine, the sourer they will become.

Grape leaves can be used as an edible wrap. Here's a recipe for doing just that!

Stuffed Grape Leaves with Herbed Rice

INGREDIENTS

- 3 cups water
- 1 ½ cups white or brown rice
- 2 cloves of garlic (or one teaspoon of garlic powder)
- ½ cup sassafras leaves, finely chopped
- 1 cup fresh oregano leaves
- ½ teaspoon salt
- 15 tender grape leaves
- ½ cup finely chopped onion
- ½ cup olive oil
- ¼ cup sunflower seeds (hulled)
- 1 cup Colby Jack cheese
- ¼ cup raisins
- 1 cup vegetable or chicken stock

INSTRUCTIONS

To prepare grape leaves for stuffing, drop them in boiling water until the color changes. Drain leaves. Remove the leaves from the stems of the oregano and discard the stems.

Prepare the rice. In a 1 ½ quart saucepan with a well-fitting lid, combine water, rice, garlic, sassafras, oregano, and salt.

Bring to a boil and cook until the rice is tender (depending on the type used, see package for directions)

Add a dollop of butter. Use half of the rice for stuffing and the rest for a side dish. Serve hot.

In a skillet under medium heat, sauté the onion in olive oil then add sunflower seeds, cheese, raisins, and rice mixture

Place one tablespoon of rice mixture in the center of each grape leaf and wrap the leaf around the rice. Loosely fold the bottom up toward the top and then either side to the middle of the leaf to pocket the rice.

When all of the leaves are stuffed, place them seam down in a skillet with a tight-fitting lid. Cover leaves with stock. Bring to a low simmer and cook for thirty minutes.

Serve with additional rice on the side. Feeds a family of eight.

Huckleberry or wild lowbush blueberries (Vaccinium pallidum syn. V. vacillans) also Deerberry (Vaccinium stamineum)

The name "huckleberry" may be about any number of different berry-producing plants including blueberries, bilberries European blueberries under several species of the genus Vaccinium), and whortleberries. commonly known as box huckleberry or box-leaved whortleberry, is a low North American shrub related to the blueberry and the other huckleberries.

Here in the Ozarks, we have two very common varieties the first one is known as the lowbush blueberry (Vaccinium pallidum syn. V. vacillans)

The lowbush blueberry is a stiffly branching shrub up to 3 feet high. The berries are tasty raw or cooked in pies, muffins, and preserves. It often grows in extensive colonies.

The second is the deerberry (Vaccinium stamineum). The deerberry is an irregularly branched shrub, rarely more than 6 feet high. This blueberry relative also bears edible blueberry fruits.

Black and Blue Berry Jelly

INGREDIENTS

To make juice you will need four and a half cups of blackberries and huckleberries (total) and four cups of water.

3 3/4 cups juice,

4 1/2 cups sugar, one box dry pectin,

1/2 teaspoon butter (optional)

INSTRUCTIONS

Lightly mash berries and cook in water on top of the stove for about 20 mins over medium/med-high heat. Strain berries through cheesecloth, wire mesh strainer, or sieve. SAVE JUICE! Discard berries and seeds. Measure sugar exactly. (Do not reduce or use sugar substitutes) Set aside.

Measure juice exactly. Place juice and pectin in a 6-to-8-quart sauce pot. Add butter now (if using) to reduce foaming. On high heat, bring the mixture to a full rolling boil. (a boil that will not stop bubbling when stirred) on high heat, STIR CONSTANTLY!

Stir in all of the sugar. Return to a rolling boil and boil for exactly one minute, Stirring constantly. Remove from heat and skim off any foam.

Quickly ladle into prepared jars, within 1/8 inch of the top. Wipe jar rims and threads with a damp cloth. Cover with two-piece lids. Screw on tightly.

Process in a hot water bath for 5 mins or use the inversion method. Save any leftover juice for a second batch! You can add up to 1/2 cup of water to juice if needed to make exact measurements.

Red Mulberries (Morus rubra)

If you're lucky enough to have a mulberry tree nearby, you have a delicious non-thorny alternative to blackberries earlier in the season. This Ozark native plant, unlike blackberries, grow on trees and they are enjoyed by humans and animals alike. This past summer I discovered that I had a mulberry tree in my yard, and I also discovered that squirrels loved them almost as much as I did.

If the squirrels hadn't gotten them, I would have spread out a cotton sheet under the mulberry tree and given the tree a shake. The fruit would have fallen onto the sheet. I would have picked up the berries and used them in pies or cobblers like I do blackberries. Well, maybe next year. . .

Passionflower, Purple (passiflora incarnata)

Here's a native, showy flower with lots of potential. The more common name here in the Ozarks is Maypop. The edible parts include fruits, buds, flowers, leaves, and seeds, prepared in various ways according to your passions. 'Why "Maypops"? If you absent-mindedly step on one of these round fruits as you are busily foraging, it will sound off a loud POP underfoot.

To eat the fruit of passionflower, you can crunch the whole fruit, seeds, and all, or spit out the seeds as you partake of the sweet citrusy fruit. Flowers are quite edible raw as well and taste lovely in salads. Young fruits can be boiled like new potatoes, and the leaves steeped as a calming tea. Strain the juice from the seeds to make an acceptable jelly or wine. A bonus characteristic is that the flowers are loved by butterflies.

Here's a recipe for maypop jelly.

Maypop Jelly

INGREDIENTS

3 cups thawed frozen passion fruit pulp
1-1/2 cups water
1 box Fruit Pectin
1/2 tsp. butter or margarine
6 cups sugar, measured into a separate bowl

INSTRUCTIONS

Bring boiling-water canner, half full of water, to simmer. Wash jars and screw bands in hot soapy water; rinse with warm water. Pour boiling water over the lids in a saucepan off the heat. Let stand in hot water until ready to use. Drain well before filling.

Combine fruit pulp and water in 6- or 8-qt. saucepot. Stir in pectin. Add butter to reduce foaming. Bring mixture to a full rolling boil on high heat and stir constantly. Now, stir in sugar. Return mixture to a full rolling boil and boil for exactly 1 min, continuing to stir constantly. Remove from heat. Skim off any foam with a metal spoon.

Ladle immediately into prepared jars, filling to within 1/4 inch of tops. Wipe jar rims and threads. Cover with two-piece lids. Screw bands tightly. Place jars on an elevated rack in the canner.

Lower rack into canner. (Water must cover jars by 1 to 2 inches. Add boiling water, if necessary.) Cover; bring water to a gentle boil. Process 10 min.

***

Passion Fruit Cordial

INGREDIENTS

1 cup passion fruit pulp (seeds and all)
3/4 cup organic cane sugar or honey
3 cups water
1 tsp citric acid or 1 tablespoon lemon juice
Add all ingredients to a large canning jar and stir vigorously until sugar is dissolved.

INSTRUCTIONS

Place a paper towel or linen cloth over the mouth of the jar and secure it with a rubber band. Keep in a cool indoor location (NOT in the refrigerator) and out of the sun.

Stir vigorously with a clean spoon for 30 seconds *at least* once per day and ideally twice per day, once in the morning and once in the evening. Taste a small amount each time after stirring to measure flavor and bubble development. Within 3-4 days, you'll start to notice the concoction starts to bubble and a bit of foam begins to develop on top because native yeasts have begun to colonize it, kickstarting the fermentation process. After 7-10 days your cordial should be ready. Bottle and store in the fridge for up to 3-6 months. Enjoy in nice small glasses-Cheers!

Pawpaw (Asimina triloba)

Pawpaws grow in thickets in the forest understory and along woodland edges. It is the native plant that produces the largest berry in North America. The tree has a semi-tropical appearance and is known for its fruit, the largest berry (up to 5 inches long) produced by any tree native to the United States. The fruit is nutritious and has been used in cancer therapy. Its twigs and bark have a natural insecticide.

These plants naturally thrive in wettish areas like river bottoms, but their range has expanded into higher and drier forests in recent years. Pawpaw's flavor is a cross between banana, mango, and pineapple. I find that it has more of the texture and flavor of the banana although there is a natural bitterness to the fruit. This slight bitterness is caused by a thin layer of phenolic compounds that lies between the skin and the sweet flesh. Simply scrape away that layer from the flesh to avoid the bitterness.

The banana flavor gives it some of its nicknames including poor man's banana and Indiana banana. Other nicknames include Billy the Kid and Bandango.

Pawpaw fruits are normally three to six inches long, sort of kidney-shaped, and grow in clusters like bananas. The pawpaw fruits start off green (often with black spots) and turn yellow, brown, and then purplish black. They get super-soft and fall off the tree when they're fully ripe, but they can be shaken off when they're close to being ripe. It's wise to pick them earlier rather than later because, here in the Ozarks, the fruit is ready for harvest sometime during October. You're competing with raccoons, possums, squirrels, and any manner of fruit-eating animals that share a habitat with pawpaw, and once the fruit is ripe, it falls off the tree. This occurs earlier in the northern regions and later in the southern parts of this region.

Pawpaw has a distinct floral or fruity smell which alludes to the sweet flesh that lies beneath the skin. The skin, which is not eaten, is thin but tough and bruises easily — it's a quality that usually gets blamed for the pawpaw's failure to achieve commercial status in modern markets. The light-yellow flesh inside is mushy and tends to ooze out of the skin when you cut the pawpaw open.

It's not a fruit that you just take a bite of because they have big, black, and hard seeds. These large dark brown seeds are toxic and must be separated from the pulp along with the skin leaving just the pulp for eating.

You can eat the pulp straight from picking them (or you can pick them green and allow them to ripen) Here's a recipe for bread made from pawpaw that tastes like banana bread.

Pawpaw Bread

(If you like banana bread, you'll love pawpaw bread)

INSTRUCTIONS

Cream together:
½ cup vegetable oil
⅔ cup white sugar
2 beaten eggs,
1 ¼ cup of pawpaw pulp

INSTRUCTIONS

Mix dry ingredients together:
1 ¾ cup of all-purpose flour
2 ¼ teaspoons baking powder
½ teaspoon salt
Preheat the oven to 350 degrees F.
Blend dry ingredients into wet ingredients, and mix until smooth.

Add optional ½ cup of chopped nuts.

Pour batter into an 8 ½ by 4 ½ inch greased and floured bread pan and bake for about an hour or until done.

If you happen to be lucky enough to find enough pawpaw, the fruit pulp will keep in the freezer. Remove the skins and the seeds and store them in a freezer bag. I recommend storing just enough in each bag to make a single loaf of pawpaw bread.

Common American Persimmons (Diospyros virginiana)

Caution: *They're delicious fresh but go easy until you know how your belly reacts if you know what I mean. Lots of fiber here!*

The Latin name for persimmon literally means "Fruit of the Gods." The American persimmon was relished by Native Americans but has never been embraced as a commercial fruit crop because most cultivars are too soft for commercial shipping. This fruit is high in nutrients like vitamin C and calcium.

The American persimmon is cold hardy. Persimmon trees are usually either male or female, but some have complete flowers that make them self-fruitful. They are somewhat unique in that sexual expression can vary from year to year. Trees stay dormant longer than most fruit trees, and blossoming is relatively late in the season and rarely damaged by late-spring frosts.

American persimmons are bitterly sour until they are thoroughly ripe. The unripe fruit is extremely astringent and if you've ever eaten unripe persimmon, you'd understand why they say, "It puckered me up like a green persimmon." However, when ripened the fruit is sweet and delicious (though some may not like the soft, pudding-like texture). Persimmons can be eaten cooked into pies, cookies, or cakes, dried, or simply eaten fresh., Native Americans used them in gruel, cornbread, and pudding. Be sure to try our recipe for persimmon cake or persimmon pudding.

Persimmon Cake

INGREDIENTS

1 Stick (8 Tbsp) Butter at room temperature

1 1/3 Cup Sugar
2 Cups Persimmon Puree
1/2 Cup Milk
3 Eggs
2 Cups Flour
1 tsp Baking Powder
1/4 tsp Baking Soda
1 tsp Salt
1 tsp Cinnamon
1/8 tsp Nutmeg

INSTRUCTIONS

Preheat the oven to 350 F, grease and flour a 9X13 baking dish,

Cream together the butter and sugar until light,

Add eggs, milk, and persimmon puree, gently folding in until smooth and creamy.

In a separate bowl, combine dry ingredients,

Slowly blend the dry mixture into the persimmon mixture

Spoon into the prepared cake pan and bake for one hour, or until a toothpick inserted into the center comes out clean. Great with a bunch of whipped cream on top, warm or cold!

***

Old Fashioned Persimmon Pudding

INGREDIENTS

cooking spray
4 cups all-purpose flour
1 teaspoon baking soda
1 teaspoon baking powder
½ teaspoon salt

1 teaspoon cinnamon

1 cup white sugar

1 cup brown sugar

3 eggs, beaten.

2 cups milk

2 ½ cups persimmon pulp

6 tablespoons butter

INSTRUCTIONS

Preheat oven to 300 degrees F (150 degrees C). Spray a 9x13-inch baking dish with cooking spray.

In a bowl, whisk together the flour, white sugar, brown sugar, baking soda, baking powder, salt, and cinnamon, until thoroughly combined. In a large bowl, beat the eggs and milk together until smooth, and add the flour mixture, alternating with the persimmon pulp in several additions, mixing well after each addition. Stir in the melted butter. Scrape the batter into the prepared baking dish.

Bake in the preheated oven until a toothpick inserted into the pudding comes out clean, about 1 hour. Allow it to cool.

Wild Plums (Prunus Americana)

There are many species within this genus. Some are native to the Ozarks like the Chickasaw plum (P. (P. angustifolia), wild goose plum (P. hortulana), Mexican plum, (P. mexicana). Wild plums are shrubs that propagate by root sprouts to form thickets, or they can be small trees with spreading low-hanging branches. It is popular for its ornamental appearance, edible fruit, and its benefit to wildlife.

Several years ago, I lived on a farm that had a field of wild plum trees. They have pretty clusters of smooth fragrant flowers in the spring. These plums have fruited, globe-shaped pinkish fruit that ripens in July, just after the blackberry season has ended. Because the skin was tough, I found that removing the seeds and then running them through my mechanical strainer made a juice that I was able to make into jelly and plum sauce for sweet and sour chicken.

At least eleven species in the genus Prunus have been recorded growing in natural settings in the Ozarks, and at least four of them are called "plums." The rest are cherries and peaches.

Black cherry, wild cherry, or rum cherry (Prunus serotina)

Black cherry is a common tree in the Ozarks. I have several of these in the fence row between my property and the neighbors. This native of the Ozarks usually grows 32–50 feet high. Dense, cylindrical, many-flowered flower clusters 3–6 inches long develop after the leaves develop.

Other Stone Fruit

You may also find cultivated fruits in old homesites **like sour cherry (Prunus cerasus), perfumed cherry (P. mahaleb), wild peach and nectarine (Prunus. persica),** These cultivated fruit trees originated in Eurasia. but sometimes escapes from cultivation or persists at old home sites.

These fruits are not only excellent in jellies, jams, and various sauces but also are great for making fruit leather. To make fruit leather using these fruits, combine the pulp of any one of these fruits with an equal amount of applesauce and sweetened to taste, spread out on drying trays in a food dehydrator, and allow them to dry until they come out in sheets. These will last several months in the cupboard this way.

You can also dry the fruit for dried fruit. Simply remove the stones and dry them in your food dehydrator until they reach a raisin-like consistency. Store them in moisture-proof containers.

~ 4 ~

OZARK FORAGABLE VEGETABLES

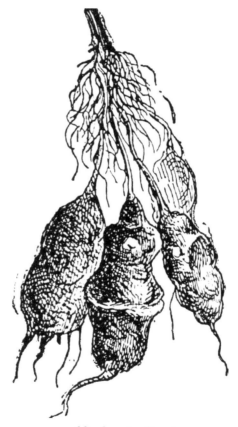

public domain clipart

Ostrich Fern Fiddleheads (Matteuccia struthiopteris)

Caution: *Some fern fiddlehead varieties contain the carcinogenic compound ptaquiloside, which causes DNA damage, thus leading to cancers of the digestive tract. Spores from them have also been implicated as carcinogens.*

Fiddlehead ferns or fiddlehead greens taste like a cross between asparagus, baby spinach, and artichoke. They have a grassy, spring-like flavor with a touch of nuttiness. Fiddleheads can be a healthful addition to your diet packed with antioxidants, omega acids, iron, and fiber.

These furled fronds of a young fern can be harvested for use as a vegetable. They have been eaten by many cultures throughout history, either fresh, cooked, or pickled.

Harvest them early in the season before the frond has opened and reached its full height, they are cut close to the ground and if left on the plant, each fiddlehead would unroll into a new frond. As fiddleheads are harvested early in the season before the frond has opened and reached its full height, they are cut close to the ground.

Ostrich fern fiddleheads (Matteuccia struthiopteris) are the most popular for foraging, as they are the tastiest (and edible). You'll find them in the Ozarks near streams and moist, forested areas. Many Native American tribes would traditionally harvest fiddleheads, and these days they are even commercially harvested in the spring.

Because some types of ferns contain ptaquiloside, be certain that you know what type of fern fiddleheads you are collecting.

Ptaquiloside is water-soluble and destroyed by cooking and in alkaline conditions created by soaking The fiddleheads can be soaked in water and ash to detoxify the plant before eating. Using alum or grape leaves placed in cold water to soak will degenerate the toxins. These toxins degenerate at room temperature and denature almost completely at boiling temperature. Despite this, only consume these in moderation to reduce the chances of cancer formation.

Some varieties of uncooked fiddleheads contain the enzyme thiaminase, which breaks down thiamine (vitamin B1). Excessive consumption of uncooked fiddleheads can lead to vitamin B1 deficiency (beriberi), especially in animals with simple stomachs (like ours). Ruminants (like cattle) are less vulnerable because they synthesize thiamine. Therefore, a good rule to follow is to always cook fiddlehead ferns before consuming them.

That said, if I haven't scared you off, here are a couple of cooked recipes to try.

Spring Fiddleheads

INGREDIENTS

2 pounds of fiddlehead ferns

1/2 cup (1 stick) butter

4 cloves garlic, minced (or ½ cup of fresh chopped wild garlic chives)

2 tablespoons minced shallots (or ½ cup of chopped chives)

(You can use one cup of fresh wild garlic greens and chives in place of

2 tablespoons lemon juice

Salt and pepper, to taste

INSTRUCTIONS

Blanch cleaned, fiddleheads in a large pot of lightly salted water for about 1 minute. Drain and rinse under cold water. Heat the butter in a skillet and sauté the garlic and shallots until aromatic but not browned. Add fiddleheads and sauté another 1 to 2 minutes. Season with lemon juice and salt and pepper and serve immediately.

***

Cream of Fiddlehead Soup

INGREDIENTS

1-1/2 cups fiddleheads, cleaned and finely chopped

2 tablespoons butter

2 cubes of chicken bouillon or 2 teaspoons of chicken bouillon granules or one cup of chicken stock

1 small onion, minced (or ½ cup of chives)

1 clove garlic, minced (or one cup of wild garlic greens)

2 cups milk

2 cups heavy cream

(Can use a quart of half and half instead of the milk and heavy cream)

salt and freshly ground black pepper, to taste.

INSTRUCTIONS

Steam the fiddleheads for 10 to 12 minutes, or until tender. Set it aside.

In a saucepan, melt the butter and bouillon cubes over medium heat. Add the fiddleheads, onions, and garlic, and cook for 10 minutes. Add the milk, stir often, and heat thoroughly. Add the cream, stir to incorporate, and season with salt and pepper.

Serve hot.

Garlic, Wild (allium species)

Wild garlic goes by any number of names, including ramsons, buckrams, bear's garlic, devil's garlic, gypsy's onions, and stinking

Jenny. This perennial relative of chives grows wild in damp woodlands and is often found in marshlands. Here in the Ozarks, we see them primarily during cool damp early spring or late fall months. They are often the first green you'll see in the spring and one of the last ones you'll see in the fall.

Be aware that there is a false garlic (Nothoscordum bivalve). It looks like wild garlic, but if you pick a leaf and smell it, it doesn't smell like garlic.

True garlic, of course, smells like garlic. Once you're sure that you have a true garlic plant, it can be eaten and used in any way you would use garlic or some of its other allium cousins. In addition to the garlic bulb, which also tends to be small, you can eat the tender greens like you would chives. Later, you can take the flower stem called a "scape" and use that in cooking Scapes can be added to scrambled eggs or frittatas, tossed into pasta dishes and stir-fries, simmered in soups, or added to soups. They can also be used in a pesto in place of basil or other herbs, or a sauce for a background hint of garlic. The flowers are also edible and can be added to a salad. You can also dry any part of the garlic plant to use later when fresh garlic is not available.

For a tasty dressing to go with your fresh spring green salad, give garlic scape dressing a try.

Garlic Scape Dressing

INGREDIENTS

2 garlic scapes, coarsely chopped.

2 green onions coarsely chopped (or a half cup of fresh chives)

1 teaspoon honey

2 teaspoons Dijon mustard

1/4 cup cider vinegar

1 tablespoon lemon juice

1 pinch of salt
1/8 teaspoon black pepper
1/2 cup olive oil

INSTRUCTIONS

In a blender, combine the garlic scapes, onions, honey, mustard, red wine vinegar, lemon juice, salt, and pepper. Blend until smooth.

With the blender on low, slowly add the olive oil until well blended.

Store the garlic scape dressing in an airtight container in the refrigerator for up to a week if needed. Shake before using.

Morel Mushrooms ((Morchella esculenta)

Caution: *Many species of mushrooms in Missouri are edible, but proper identification is essential to avoid illness and even death by toxic mushrooms. Some mushrooms can also be toxic to some people and not to others.*

Foraging for food education in the Ozarks would not be complete without including mushrooms. Morels (Morchella esculenta) are highly sought after here in the Ozarks. they start appearing when the days are above sixty degrees F. and nights are around forty degrees F. Morels appear when the soil is between 45 and 50 degrees. They are usually first found on south-facing slopes and then later they can be picked from north-facing hillsides. Look for them around trees such as sycamore, elm, ash, apple trees, and dead and dying trees. They like the loamy soil of the creek bottoms but will appear anywhere even in gravel and under pine trees. They are often found in burn sites and logging sites as well. If you're not sure a mushroom is a morel, don't eat it!

Eastern Prickly Pear (Opuntia humifusa formerly O. compressa)

While most prickly pears are native to warmer climates in the US, we do have a variety or two that survive Missouri winters, you'll need a good pair of leather gloves, or better yet, long BBQ tongs (Grannies' Secret: your gloves will likely be ruined because of embedded spines & hairs. How are you going to get them out?) to harvest the cactus pads, called nopales. (No-PAH-lays). They have noticeable spines and appear to be smooth in between. But tiny hair-like spines lurk, and will immediately attach to your fingers, being almost impossible to remove. However, if you follow caution, once gathered, use long tongs to roast over a flame to burn off the spines. Peel them to create tasty dishes. Slice them thin and use them like green beans. Try roasting the peeled pads over a campfire. Prickly pear can be pickled using a standard dill pickle recipe. They can also be deep-fried.

Prickly pears have a fruit, commonly called the Indian fig or Indian. tuna. These pulpy red fruits ripen in late summer, are edible, and are most often being used to make candies and jam. This fruit sits atop the pad and is quite prickly as well. It also has tiny, barbed hairs so again, use your tongs or gloves to handle them. Roast to remove the spines and then peel by using a sharp knife to slice off both ends. Next, slice through just through skin lengthwise and peel, using your fingers. Even though they have small hard seeds that you'll have to spit out, they are sweet and worth the effort. They taste like melons. If you find you enjoy them, think about growing them as part of your native plant gardens in our Ozark dry, rocky soil.

Common Thistle stems (Cirsium vulgare)

There are many varieties, this one is the bull thistle also known as the common thistle.

While beautiful, this is on the invasive weed list in many states, and widespread in Missouri. The early leaves can be cooked as a potherb. You can also prepare the young bloom shoots by wearing gloves while you snip off leaves and spines. Peel the outer rind from the stem, cut it into 3-inch sections, boil, and eat like an artichoke (dip in butter and pull stems through teeth, discarding stringy part). Sounds pretty tasty, and you'll be doing your part in helping to control this pesky plant.

Common Burdock (Arctium minus)

Though not original to the Ozarks, burdock has been naturalized to this area and other parts of the world and has become a weed. I have a patch of it in my yard that I have to keep under control.

Burdock root, which is commonly eaten in Japan, and some parts of Europe, and is becoming more popular in the U.S., is a source of inulin, a type of prebiotic fiber that feeds the good bacteria in the large intestine to improve digestion.

You can find fresh burdock root at natural food stores and if you're lucky, farmers' markets. When eating it, peel the outer layer. Eat it raw or cooked by sautéing or stir-frying.

Cattail (Typha spp.)

Caution: *Avoid eating cattails from bodies of water that are polluted with lead or pesticide residues.*

Cattails are among the first wetland plants to colonize areas of newly exposed wet mud, with their abundant wind-dispersed seeds. Buried seeds can survive in the soil for long periods and here in the Ozarks, cattails can be found in and around different types of water sources.

We can eat many parts of the cattail and parts of it can be eaten throughout the year making it a year-round forageable food. The tender shoots of the cattail that come before the plant flowers can be squeezed and eaten raw or cooked. The shoots growing from the roots can be picked and eaten raw. Harvested in the fall to early spring, the rhizomes or "roots" can be eaten, and the protein they have is compared in nutritional value to corn or rice. These "roots" can be dried and made into flour. The underground tuber-shaped part of the plant can be peeled and eaten raw or cooked like a potato.

The skin of the young stems can be peeled off and the tender white inside can be eaten raw. They can also be boiled and eaten like asparagus. In the late spring, the bases of the leaves can be eaten raw or cooked.

The sheath can be removed from the developing flower spike and boiled and eaten like corn on the cob. In mid-summer, the pollen can be collected and used as a flour supplement or thickener.

Waterlilies. White (Nymphaea odorata,)

Another water plant that can often be found in ponds around old farmsteads is waterlilies. These are relatively easy to identify in that they live in the water, have big leaves, and produce beautiful magnolia-like blossoms.

The spongy roots of this wild vegetable can be found in the winter and can make a satisfying meal by itself. The forage that is both spongy and buoyant enough to float is both tender and tasty when prepared properly.

The stems beneath the lily pads are thick and can be six feet long and as thick as a softball is round and are covered with brown skin and eyes or sprouting points like are in potatoes. Stalks and flower stems grow from these eyes.

The leaves can be harvested by wading out into a patch and pulling them loose, stalk, and all. When you've gathered a half dozen of the large pads and stems, wash them well with lots of running water to remove all debris and harbored insects.

Once the leaves are washed, with a large knife, cut them into pieces and use them for pond lily soup.

Pond Lily Soup

INGREDIENTS

1 pound venison roast (cheap cuts of beef also work well)
5-6 strips of bacon chopped,
2 handfuls of pond lily leaves
Any cooked vegetables you want to add that you have on hand like potatoes, turnips, carrots, onion, or garlic.

INSTRUCTIONS

Simmer one pound of venison (deer) roast for about an hour or until it gets tender. Chop it up and add several pieces of chopped bacon and cook for another hour.

When the meat is tender, remove it from the fire, allow it to cool, and put two handfuls of pond lily leaves and any other vegetables you might have on hand in with the meat. Cook until the leaves are tender and season with salt and pepper.

***

Other Ways to Eat Pond Lily

Other parts of the pond lily are also tasty. Boil unopened buds, for a minute in salted water or steamed and served with melted butter or yogurt.

Pickle the flower buds. Pick unopened flowers along with one sprig of dill and a fresh or dried red cayenne pepper and pack them into sterilized one-quart canning jars. On the stove, boil together one cup of white vinegar, ¼ cup of salt, and ½ teaspoon of alum. Pour the solution over the contents of the jar and fill the rest of the water that you've boiled for more than a minute. Seal and let stand for two months. Enjoy when cold winds are blowing and you're lookin' for a taste of spring!

Pond lily buds, flowers, and leaves can be wilted in bacon grease or olive oil just like you can most any green. Just cut them into bite-sized pieces and stir the hot grease until they're well-coated and brown at the edges.

You can eat pond lily roots by pulling them up and peeling them with a very sharp knife to remove the outer layer and the eyes. Cut the white root into thick slices and boil the pieces several times and discard the water between each time you boil them. Adding vinegar to the water helps neutralize the bitterness. The prepared sections of the root can be baked, fried, or cooked in soup.

A good way to bake pond lily root is to take a medium-sized baking dish and place processed slices into it. Add two tablespoons of butter. Sprinkle with salt and add ¾ cup of potato water (water from cooking potatoes). Cover with parboiled pond lily leaves and bake at 375 degrees Fahrenheit for about twenty-five minutes. Serve hot.

Jerusalem Artichoke (Helianthus tuberosus)

I was first introduced to Jerusalem artichokes before my middle son was born. Their earthy flavor reminds me of water chestnuts, so I started using them in place of water chestnuts in stir fry.

These irregular-shaped tubers can be used in place of many recipes calling for potatoes. Fried, mashed, baked, or raw in salads. These gems can be included in your dill pickle recipe as well. You'll find them in moist areas, waste ground such as roadsides, or perhaps railroad rights of way. They also transplant easily into your home garden. Just know their high inulin content can make some people "quite windy".

Jerusalem artichokes are low on the glycemic index, so they are an excellent way of controlling blood sugar. Plus, they are a tasty substitute for potatoes when you're wanting more carbohydrates.

Orange Daylily (Hemerocallis fulva)

Orange Day Lilies ((Hemerocallis fulva) are very delicious. For centuries, daylilies have been a staple food in many parts of Asia and have become naturalized in many parts of the Ozarks including my flower garden.

Do take time to learn about and enjoy Mother Nature's grocery store! In addition to harvesting daylily greens mentioned back in Greens, (pages 29-30) daylilies can be harvested three more times during the year. There are so many ways to cook these up, an entire volume could be devoted to daylily cuisine!

You can eat the unopened flower buds. Simply put, try picking the unopened bud and boil for a couple of minutes. They resemble tender green beans or asparagus at this stage- a meal not to be sneezed at!

A little later in the week, the unopened flowers are delicious fritter material. Any good fritter recipe will do, but here is a simple one.

Fritter Recipe

INGREDIENTS

1 cup flour
1 cup beer
¼ teaspoon salt
1 tablespoon corn or olive oil.

INSTRUCTIONS

Stir this batter and let it sit for 30 minutes before dipping the clean flowers into the batter, then into a deep skillet of hot oil until golden brown. Drain and try a dusting of sugar.

After all, that good eating, don't overlook the day-old, wilted flowers. If there are still any flowers left these wilted flowers can be added as thickening to any soup or stew.

Finally, underground, the small edible tubers await your discovery! They can be dug year-round if the ground isn't frozen. Raw, cooked with butter, or dried and ground into flour, just experiment.

Hint: freeze some or all of the above for winter use.

(Remember there's more about eating daylily greens in Forageable Greens on pages 29-30.

~ 5 ~

OZARK FORGEABLE NUTS

public domain clipart

When Good Fences Made Good Neighbors

Old fence lines are often strung with trees "sort of line of sight" acting as fence posts. Nowadays, some rely on lawyers and surveyors to determine property lines, but that wasn't always the case.

In times past here in the Ozarks, there was little doubt who owned the fence and was responsible for its upkeep. If the fencing staples were on your side of the fenceposts and faced your property, the fence was your responsibility to maintain. If the staples faced the opposite direction, your neighbor was responsible for that maintenance.

A friend of mine also says that this is the way it is with fence lines in the Ozarks.

"When standing in the middle of the perimeter fence you share with your neighbor, all the fence to your right is your responsibility, that to the left is your neighbor's", according to Missouri's fence law.

This was an important fact when animals got through a poorly maintained fence. If, for instance, your neighbor's pig escaped and got into your garden and the fence was your responsibility to maintain, you could be out of luck because it could be considered your own fault. However, if your neighbor was expected to maintain the fence, you could expect damage to the garden.

The bottom line is, just be friendly with your neighbors. Most of the time a neighbor is only as nice a person as you are to them. You might end up with the pig, and you'uns might just like to share the ornery pig barbecued!

Along fence lines, you'll find many trees and many of them are nut trees. One of the most common are members of the oak family.

White oak acorns (Quersus species)

You're apt to find a lot of trees along your fence line and many of them are likely to be nut trees, and especially oak trees. Twenty-two species of oaks are native or have been naturalized in the Ozarks. In addition, more than thirty different oak hybrids (crosses between the various species) have been recorded. There are two basic types, the red oak group, and the white oak group.

The red oak group, (Lobatae or sometimes called Erythrobalanus), is famous for leaves with jagged, bristle-tipped teeth or lobes and "bitter" acorns that take two years to mature. The most famous representatives of this group are the different species of red oak and black oak, Q. velutina. Eating acorns from these trees is especially bitter and not recommended.

The white oak group, (Quercus or sometimes called Leucobalanus), is famous for having leaves with rounded lobes and "sweet" acorns that mature in a single year. The white oak (Q. alba) is the most famous species in this group. These are the ones that are recommended for making acorn flour or meal.

Here's how to tell if an oak tree is a red oak or a white oak. Red oak leaves have bristle-tipped lobes or teeth on their leaves (or, in species whose leaves are both unlobed and untoothed, a bristle appears at least on the leaf tip). White oak leaves lack bristle tips and look rounded. Red oak bark is often dark gray, brown, or occasionally black, and it is rough, hard, and ridged. White oak bark is a lighter color and is scaly or flaky. Red oak acorns are more bitter, and they mature in two seasons. You'll see two age groups of acorns on single twigs in summer, and there are immature acorns present on the tree during winter. White oak acorns are sweet, and they mature on the tree in a single growing season. The white oaks typically germinate immediately after falling from the tree. So, if you see only one age group of acorns on the tree in the summer, and no immature acorns in the winter, that tree is a white oak tree rather than a red oak.

You'll want to make flour or ground meal out of the white oak acorns. It's a lot of work, but if you want to stretch your white flour, you can use a cup of acorn flour to a cup of white flour thereby extending your storebought flour twice as far.

First, you'll want to gather acorns. Choose only the best acorns. Gather acorns that don't have caps attached (these were rejected by the tree and not suitable) or acorns with holes in them (insect damage) Gather only white oak acorns rather than acorns from other types of oak trees.

The easiest way to leach your acorns is by using the cold leach method. First, dry your acorns in a dehydrator for about 24 hours to ensure that they are completely dry.

Next, crack the nuts and remove the nutmeats. Discard the shells. Now, remove the skins (also known as testa). This should be easy to do with white oak acorns (much easier than with red oak acorns). Next, grind the nuts.

Once the acorns are ground, leach the tannins from the acorns by adding three parts of water to one part of the acorns and allow to set for 24 hours. After the 24 hours are up, drain water from the ground acorns and set for another 24 hours. Continue this process for several days until the acorns no longer taste bitter. You'll know when the leaching is done if when you taste the water, the bitterness is gone.

Strain the mash through a colander and be sure to save the liquid. The liquid is a form of nut milk at this point which you can use in cooking or even drinking so you'll want to strain out any remaining acorn residue with a paper filter and use it.

Take the clay-like paste that stays and dry it, again in the dehydrator. You can store dried acorn meal in the refrigerator or freezer if you don't plan to use the meal immediately.

However, unprocessed nuts can be stored for months without going bad if you store them in a tightly sealed container in a cool dry location.

Hickory Nut (Carya spp.)

Most hickory nut trees produce small nuts, and we Ozarkians call them "pig nuts", but don't let this make you think that they are just pig food. They are a valuable resource. If you find a quality-producing tree, keep yours a secret.

Six species of hickory grow naturally in the Ozarks. There are true hickories like shagbark (C. ovata), mockernut (C. tomentosa), pignut (C. glabra), and black hickory (Ozark pignut hickory) (C. texana). In the Ozarks, there are also pecan hickories which include pecan (C. illinoinensis), and bitternut (C. cordiformis).

Hickory nuts are edible nuts with a slightly sweet and nutty taste. They look and taste like pecans. Hickory nuts are primarily a source of fat, but they also have moderate amounts of carbohydrates and protein. They supply a wide range of vitamins and minerals. They can be used to replace pecans in many recipes. You'll want a quart fruit jar, a pair of safety glasses, a stout rock, and a hammer, but cracking nuts is a pleasant way to spend the afternoon.

American Hazelnuts (Corylus americana)

In the Ozarks, hazelnuts are ready to harvest in July-August. The shells or bracts are more or less flat, unlobed, leafy to paper in texture, completely enclosing the nut and falling with it; each bract projects far beyond the nut, is strongly veined, felty-hairy, with the outer edge sharply toothed. The nuts are egg- to globe-shaped, usually wider than long, and the shell is thick and hard. The nuts are light brown, sweet, and edible.

Pawpaw Hazelnut Acorn Pancakes

INGREDIENTS

1 cup pawpaw pulp, (or 1 very ripe banana)

½ cup whole wheat pastry flour (or all-purpose flour)
1 tablespoon baking powder
1/8 teaspoon salt
1/3 cup acorn flour (or cornmeal)
¾ cup milk
1 large egg
½ cup of chopped hazelnuts
Vegetable oil for brushing the griddle

INSTRUCTIONS

Combine all ingredients except hazelnuts and vegetable oil in your food processor. Add chopped hazelnuts.

Heat the griddle over medium heat and brush with oil. Drop about ¼ cup of batter onto the griddle to form pancakes that are 4 inches in diameter. Cook until bubbles appear on the surface and the undersides are golden brown. Flip pancakes with a metal spatula and cook until the undersides are golden brown, and pancakes are fully cooked. Makes about 10 pancakes. Serve with warm maple or homemade fruit syrup.

Black Walnuts (Juglans nigra)

Black Walnut is a deciduous tree that is native to North America and a member of the walnut family. When you think of Ozark forageables, black walnuts should be one of the first things that come to mind. About 65% of the annual wild harvest comes from the state of Missouri here in the Ozarks.

Black Walnuts have been collected in the Ozarks for over a century and sold to help Ozark families make ends meet at the end of the year. Black walnuts are gathered each fall in the Ozarks and usually sold to the Hammond Black Walnut Company at various hulling stations. We might keep a few for ourselves for winter snacking.

Every part of the nut from the hull to the shell to the nut meat has many uses. More black walnuts are collected in the Ozarks than in any other region in the U.S. In our house, it's a family tradition to gather our buckets and spend October days in the beautiful autumn sunshine as we pick up "black gold."

Not to be confused with English walnuts, the black walnut has a hearty, earthier wild taste and for many can be a new taste bud discovery. Fruit is often produced irregularly where in some years they produce larger crops than others. Fruiting can begin when the tree is 4–6 years old, but large crops take 20 years. Black walnut is more resistant to frost than the English or Persian walnut but thrives best in the warmer regions of fertile, lowland soils with high water tables, although it will also grow in drier soils, but much more slowly.

American pioneers let the nuts dry in the sun, then removed the husks and let the kernels dry which makes them less bitter. Kernel extraction from the fruit of the black walnut is difficult. The thick, hard shell is tightly bound by tall ridges to a thick husk. To extract the nutmeats, rolling the nut underfoot on a hard surface such as a driveway is a common method. Some people take a thick plywood board and drill a nut-sized hole in it (from one to two inches in diameter) and smash the nut through the hole using a hammer. The nut goes through the hole and the husk remains behind. Commercial huskers use a car tire rotating against a metal mesh to accomplish this task.

For a true Ozarks treat, here's a classic!

Black Walnut Pie

INGREDIENTS

3 eggs, lightly beaten.
1 Tablespoon lemon juice
1 cup sorghum molasses (another product of the Ozarks)
1 teaspoon vanilla

1 cup white sugar

2 cups Black Walnuts

2 Tablespoons melted butter.

9″ piecrust (see piecrust recipe used for blackberry cobbler cut the recipe in half or use for two pies)

(Use the two crusts, 9-inch pie crust recipe used for the Blackberry Cobbler on pages 50-51)

INSTRUCTIONS

Preheat oven to 350°F. Prepare pie crust and put it into a 9-inch pie pan.

Gently combine all ingredients, in the order listed. Stir long enough to begin dissolving the sugar, but not enough to incorporate air into the filling. Do not beat, or the pie will have air bubbles on the top instead of Black Walnuts, spoiling the glossy look of the glazed nuts.

Pour the mixture into the unbaked pie crust. Bake on a cookie sheet for one hour or until the center of the pie is no longer gooey and the Black Walnuts are browned.

Serve either hot or cold, but for the best appearance, allow the pie to reach room temperature before cutting. No pie is complete without some whipped cream or ice cream so be sure to slap a dollop on top. Enjoy!

***

Black Walnut Turkey Breast Salad

INGREDIENTS

2 cups of Turkey breast cooked and cubed.

2 cups rotini cooked as per package.

1 cup fresh asparagus, uncooked and cut into one-inch pieces

1 cup red seedless grapes

1 cup black walnuts
¼ cup fresh chopped red peppers
Dressing:
¾ cup salad dressing or mayonnaise
¼ cup sour cream
1 tablespoon lemon juice
1 tablespoon Dijon mustard
1 teaspoon curry powder
Dash of cayenne pepper
Salt and pepper to taste.

INSTRUCTIONS

Place salad ingredients in a large bowl and toss gently. Set it aside while you make the dressing.

Mix dressing ingredients well and pour over the salad and mix gently until the dressing covers all the ingredients. Chill for several hours to allow the flavors to mingle. Serve on lettuce leaves. Makes six one-cup servings.

***

If you're lucky enough to still have black walnuts in the spring, this next recipe is a fantastic way to introduce your family to spring-foraged greens.

***

Mixed Field Greens with Toasted Black Walnuts and Honey Apple Vinaigrette

INGREDIENTS

Mixed foraged and garden greens
¼ cup black walnuts
Salt and pepper
Sliced Apples

INSTRUCTIONS

Toast black walnuts in a skillet over a low flame and sprinkle with salt and pepper. Serve warm over the mixed green salad.

Mix salad greens in a bowl and top with honey apple vinaigrette salad dressing.

***

Honey Apple Vinaigrette Salad Dressing

INGREDIENTS

¼ cup red wine vinegar
½ cup extra virgin olive oil
¼ cup applesauce
Honey to taste
Salt and pepper to taste

INSTRUCTIONS

Mix all the dressing ingredients and add only enough honey to bind the ingredients.

Assemble salad and garnish with fresh apple slices.

~ 6 ~

IT'S TIME TO SAY GOODBYE FOR NOW

Sorry to see you go. I hope you enjoyed spending time with us. As you have seen from the recipes in this book, you don't have to live like poor folk just because you're eating foods that other people consider weeds. I hope you take the time to try a few of them.

Thanks for allowing us to share with you! We're feverishly writing additional books for this series, so if you're hankering to learn more from us, we'll have more Ozark pearls of wisdom and practical observations for you d'reckly.

If you live in the Ozarks and want to share a recipe or a story (or both!) in a future book in this series, be sure to contact us through our Facebook page messenger. We'd be proud glad to hear from you.

If all you want is to learn more of what other secrets the grannies have to share, that's fine too.

Can't wait until our next book comes out? Y'all come visit us at our Facebook group *Ozark Grannies' Secrets https://www.facebook.com/groups/3242821695985077/*

Y'all come back now!

ABOUT THE OZARK GRANNIES' SECRETS AUTHORS

Cygnet Brown

Cygnet Brown currently lives in the Missouri Ozarks. She is the author of the historical fiction series *The Locket Saga.* She produced her first nonfiction book in 2013. This book, *Simply Vegetable Gardening,* is based on her 50 years of gardening experience. Among her writings are several nonfiction books including *Help from Kelp Using Diatomaceous Earth, around the House and Yard, Living Today the Power of Now, Write a Book and Ignite Your Business,* and most recently *The Survival Garden (2021).*

Kerry Kelley

Kerry Kelley is a 40-year resident and homesteader in the Missouri Ozarks. She is a lifelong gardener, forager, and self-taught Ozarks Granny. She makes her home on 110 acres with her husband.

Along with co-author Cygnet Brown, she hopes to preserve authentic Ozarks culture and customs through the Ozark Grannies' Secrets.

RESOURCES

Of course, a book this small can't possibly contain all the plants can be foraged here in the Ozarks, nor could we include all the recipes, therefore, we're sharing a list of resources to help you understand and enjoy the biodiversity here of the Ozarks even more.

Do or Die Kitchen, Edible Plants in Arkansas Foraging Guide- https://www.doordiekitchen.com/edible-plants-in-arkansas

Missouri Department of Conservation- https://mdc.mo.gov/

George O White State Forest Nursery- https://mdc.mo.gov/

Grow Native www.gonative.org/

Eating the Ozarks by Rachel West- https://eatingtheozarks.com/index.html#/

Foraging the Ozarks: Finding, Identifying, and Preparing Edible Wild Foods in the Ozarks by Bo Brown

For more about Ozarks topography here's a site with a lot of information.

United States Geological Survey USGS- https://www.usgs.gov/

INDEX

CPSIA information can be obtained
at www.ICGtesting.com
Printed in the USA
BVHW051915250423
663037BV00007B/84